SOMEWHERE IN THE DARK RECESSES

SOMEWHERE IN THE DARK RECESSES

My Personal Journey Through Schizophrenia

Nicole Levesque

Cover image by Kieferpix

This book includes many details of my own journey through schizophrenia. It is truly not a substitute for obtaining proper psychiatric advice, from your own physician. Please always consult your physician, for his or her own invaluable counsel as you travel on your own journey through schizophrenia.

ISBN: 0997841281
ISBN 13: 9780997841282
Library of Congress Control Number: 2016911731
TelaVesque Press, Stamford, Connecticut

DEDICATION

First and foremost, I would like to dedicate this book to my partner in life, who has always been there for me, during both the good and bad times. My husband is a patient, kind and loving individual. He has read many columns in various magazines and articles on the computer about the illness, just to be able to understand my outbursts and psychoses better. He is an amazing man, who I can rely upon, at any hour, of each and every day. Our message, both my husband's and my own, is to accept yourself as you are, because God made you. There is only one of you, and each of you are special.

Also, I would like to recognize and dedicate this book to Bart Sloan M.D. Being able to interpret and select the proper medications for my schizophrenia was carefully deciphered and took two years to complete. Dr. Sloan was always positive that we would arrive at the correct medications for my schizophrenia and he did indeed complete that task accurately.

Dr. Sloan, you not only figured out my medication profile, but logically calculated exactly how many milligrams of each medication that I needed for my specific illness. I am truly a lucky patient to have you as my psychiatrist. For without you, I would not have felt so good for the past fifteen years.

PREFACE

This book is an autobiography which is enmeshed with a bit of practical advice.

I wrote this book primarily for people who are suffering with schizophrenia, just as I do.

People who endure another form of mental illness, such us bipolar illness, will also find this book helpful. Additionally, others who would appreciate this book, are people that genuinely find an interest in schizophrenia, and mental illness as a whole. This includes people who know someone with a mental illness and psychiatrists who treat mental illness daily. This book takes the reader on a journey of my life, and as a result, the reader can compare what occurs in my life, to what occurs in each of their lives. I find that I take special care of my reader, since everything in the book is explained thoroughly. The first chapter is about demonstrating strange tendencies when I was a younger person. The book then moves on to what occurs during my life, until I reach the age of fifty years old, in the year 2015.

While living with this illness from such a young age, I completely knew through many experiences of my own, on how psychoses, strange thoughts, peculiar actions, and night terrors thoroughly impacted my life. Actually, I thought all of this was natural, and everyone suffered from the same difficulties as I did, when I was younger. As I grew a little older, I understood that I was different and I chose not to divulge my psychoses to anyone for a substantial period of time. Due to these repulsive interruptions which permeated my life, I never really had the time to wonder how I would feel as part of society's norm, living my life without schizophrenia.

This book, not only includes my life experiences, but it also presents vignettes from my friends at the schizophrenics anonymous meetings in chapter 8, which you can choose to read if you wish. Also, I use the pronoun he throughout the book in order to make the reading smooth, however I actually mean he or she. When I attempt to read a book, it is a daunting task for me to thoroughly concentrate and remember what I have just read.

Therefore, I have chosen a comfortably sized print for a more relaxed experience. At certain times, the text in the book may be raw, however, the story told about this illness needs to be communicated in a straightforward manner without confusion.

CONTENTS

CHAPTER 1

GROWING UP

My name is Nicole and I am a paranoid schizophrenic. I was not diagnosed until I was thirty-five years old. This was due to my reluctance in seeking out the help I needed from a psychiatrist earlier on in life. I always knew down deep inside within my soul that there was something different about me, because I had a difficult time within group situations and relating to people in general. This book will tell you about some of the odd behaviors I enacted within the past, and still go through today. Not all schizophrenic people undergo the exact same symptoms, however this is the road that I have traveled. Able to keep a journal through some of the difficult times, I was able to validate my thoughts and feelings on paper as I read them back to myself. This was extremely helpful because I was struggling to understand what was real, and what was not. Having been on antipsychotics as well as other supportive medications for about fifteen years currently, I can truly see the wonders that these medications have fulfilled in my life.

Some of my odd behaviors started when I was about three years old. I used to rock myself to sleep on a small rocking chair for hours at a time, while listening to classical music. The rocking motion soothed me and as a result I found myself going out of my body, until I eventually fell asleep. As I grew a little older, my mother noticed that I did not blend in or play with other children normally. She thought that if I were to attend a finishing school, that this would indeed help me to play with other children and avoid being the loner I had become. I always felt strange and anxious around other children, however I did seem to get along better with younger children than myself. At times, I actually bullied the younger children in order to feel more powerful and better about myself.

Other odd behaviors continued. I enjoyed walking around in a circular pattern, always in a counterclockwise direction, which also soothed me, because I was able to go out of my body which felt normal and safe. During certain times in my life as a young girl, I would sit at the dinner table, take a bite of food while getting up, walk around in a circle, and then back to my seat at the dinner table. This occurred in what seemed to be an endless amount of times. My parents said nothing to me because they were used to my many quirky behaviors. When I was in first grade, I walked into my mother's bedroom as she was sitting on her bed. I told her very nervously that I did not feel nor look like the other children in my class at school. Of course, as a concerned parent, she asked me if I wanted my hair cut or a new dress in order to make me feel better. I did not want to express myself fully, or reveal the entire truth to her because I was totally embarrassed. What I yearned to tell her was that when I looked at myself in a mirror, I saw something hideous staring back at me.

There was a large bug-like creature with an exoskeleton, comparable to a cockroach. I was ugly and I knew it. I repeated the phrase "I'm ugly" persistently. Sometimes I saw some semblance of my face, but it was greatly distorted. Some of my features were missing and others were exaggerated.

From the ages of six through to my early teens, at times I would get down on all fours, bend my head upward while looking at the ceiling and crawl. This action would give me a feeling of walking on the ceiling. Another characteristic behavior which I remember well was when I collected rocks alone for long periods of time. I especially liked the rocks with mica in them, from the open lot next door. I spent many, many hours in isolation while collecting these rocks. Actually, I should have been socializing and having fun with my friends, if I were like the other children. I was shy and attention from friends was sparse. I remember my dad was working outside in the yard one day and I was speaking with him. Meanwhile, the entire popular crowd, of about seven kids, who lived in the neighborhood, came walking down the street and immediately passed me. I shouted, "Hi guys" but not one of them responded back to me, which included the person I thought was my best friend at the time. I think that children can really sense when there is something not quite right with one of their peers, and as a result they tend to shy away from that person. Another way that I assured myself in spending time alone, was when I practiced my accordion two to three hours daily. Well, I did end up getting quite good at the classical accordion, and I was able to win second place at the United States Virtuoso competition. I was not really all that proud of myself, because this experience was more about me spending time alone practicing, instead of winning. Actually, winning over forty trophies in my life, which I accomplished, was not my goal. As a result, I just threw away my last three trophies, because they never really meant that much to me anyway. I always had trouble accepting any type of complement, because I never saw myself as anything else but a human-bug.

A couple of friends from my school would call me at home sometimes, and I just could not bring myself to answer the phone, due to the overwhelming anxiety I felt. Someone else in my family would always have to answer our phone. I also never called my friends back because I always felt as though other children were better than I was, in every respect. To this very day, I feel immediate anxiety when the phone rings. However, I do answer the phone if I am at home, and I do call people back that leave messages. My cousin from Washington State, who calls me now every Friday, tells me that I answer the phone very hesitantly, as if I am peeking around a corner. It took me many years of constantly telling myself to answer the phone, before I became more comfortable with it.

I would like to give you a sense of how I behaved in elementary Catholic school.

Being the worst acting child in the class for many grades, I was always placed with the boys, and not just with the boys but the very last student in the class because of my actions.

Getting beaten with a ruler by the nun was a daily occurrence. This was due to my talking back to the nun, which forced me to run out of the classroom and into the corridors so that the nun hopefully would not be able to catch me. I would also draw the nun with a small head and a big body or a big head with a small body; this kept me laughing for a good part of the day. I was also always passing notes to other students, because I was so bored.

Keeping my mouth quiet in school was not a task which I could complete, so I was moved to different desks in the classroom many times because I bothered everyone. One day when my teacher came back from lunch, I pulled off her veil and she was almost bald. She was very embarrassed, however, I could not stop laughing and I made her chase me for her veil for a short period of time outside. Being a bully, I needed the younger students to look up to me since I could not really make too many friends in my own class. Everyone looked at me as if I was a supreme trouble maker. Another example occurred in the winter time, when I took some packing snow, made a snowball, and threw it at a first grader's face. He ended up losing a couple of teeth and my mother had to go back to the principal's office to hear the news. Well, my parents had to pay for a couple of dental bills so they were not very happy with me.

This type of behavior, such as laughing at the teachers daily, did not disappear when I went onto high school. I was a good person down deep inside, however, things that seemed to be so very funny to me were not as funny to the rest of the class; not even in my small circle of friends. For example, my physics teacher would keep me after school because I would laugh at him while he was trying to teach. If he called me to solve a problem on the chalkboard, I acted just like he would have acted at the chalkboard and that garnered lots of laughs. That was always my goal, to acquire laughs from the other students in my class. I always did well in school, however, I had trouble concentrating and I was just more interested in laughing because that was so important to me and I do not know why.

Another time at which laughing was not appropriate occurred when my parent's home was robbed. I was about thirteen years old and for some reason I thought that this was funny. My parents, who were used to my antics, could not believe that I was laughing and kidding around, especially seeing our home in such a shambles. There are quite a few examples such as this when laughing was not apropos, however, I still made fun of people or sets of circumstances when I saw fit. Once again, I do not know why.

When I was about fifteen years old, I had a neighbor come over and he suggested that we throw rocks at my parent's house. So, we started pelting rocks at the house and I was having a great time. I should have known far better than to do what I was doing. I could have shattered a window or maybe even harmed someone coming out of the door.

My mother caught us and my neighbor fled, however, I went to see my mother, who was calling me, and she asked me why would I do such a thing? I had no answer. My parents always told me that I lacked common sense for my age and they were right.

In all of these experiences, I never really meant any harm but I never thought things through completely before I acted upon them either. I am quite a bit older now and I can see the errors of my ways. Emotionally slow for my age, I was not capable in seeing the entire picture of what I was indeed doing; whether at school or at home. I have always felt behind my peers when it came to being emotionally mature and making correct decisions for myself. Always quick to make these faulty decisions, I did not want to think about anything except what would make me happy in the moment.

When I was approximately eight to thirteen years old, at bedtime, the worse psychoses and night terrors occurred. There was one particular psychosis that I had continuously. An ugly witch on her tattered broom, flew into my bedroom almost every night, while I was awake. This scary witch and I flew to a place around my house called the mountain, where we used to play when we were young. This witch would push me off of her broomstick, and as a result I used to fall where nobody could find me, in the deep grass. I would have to walk home alone, in the dark, confronting monsters and snake-like creatures. I swore to my parents that this happened while I was awake and not while I was asleep. My parents did not seemed convinced.

In sixth grade, and for many years to come, I asked my parents how would it feel to die? God in heaven, I felt so badly inside, I just wanted to escape from reality and die. However, being brought up Catholic, I knew that I would end up in hell if I committed suicide. By the time I was fourteen years old, I spoke and thought of suicide more than just simply living my life. I was so very pained inside because of the: confusion inside of my head, distortion of normalcy, horrific night terrors and psychoses including: hearing, seeing and smelling. The voices told me to worship the devil as I was seeing him right before me.

The devil appearing before me and speaking to me remains the scariest of psychoses which I have to this day, both occurring before and after taking antipsychotic medications. I used to think about dying quite a bit so that God could take me out of my misery.

Thoughts ran through my head of what I could kill myself with and more importantly, how I would act this out. My father even asked me several times if I was using drugs during my teenage years, because of my odd behaviors. At this point in my life, I knew nothing about drugs and I told him so. Having a cousin who is paranoid schizophrenic, I asked myself sub-consciously, year after year, if I could also have this mental illness.

Being adopted by my parents, I talked myself out of the possibility of being a schizophrenic person. I was sure that I had beaten all the odds when I finally turned thirty.

I did some research on schizophrenia and I did not know, from the research I did, that one could be diagnosed so late in life. My mother told me that early on in my life, she wanted to bring me to a doctor in order to discuss my "odd behaviors". However, my father did not agree to take me because I was doing well enough in school, and besides he did see me through rose-colored glasses. I could do no wrong in his eyes. Eventually, when I did go see a psychiatrist, he told me that I had been suffering from this mental illness from an early age onward.

Before I was placed on antipsychotic medications, if someone was speaking loudly in a crowd, I felt as though they wanted to either speak with me or they were speaking derogatorily about me, which made me very upset. I usually stared at them and quietly verbalized on how I was feeling at the time. As you know, I used to play the accordion competitively. I thought that the planes which flew over my parent's house contained my competitors in them. I was sure that they wanted to check up on my progression, while I practiced the accordion for the next competition. I was convinced that there was a wire feed into my house from my competitors, so that they could hear the progress on my accordion clearly. This is known as having delusions of grandeur and some schizophrenics are known to have this. Another strange attribute was my problem of hearing where a certain sound comes from; I always seemed to pick the wrong direction from where a particular sound came from.

I was always a very structured person because I had to be. Thoughts kept running through my head so very quickly and disturbing me. Therefore, I needed some type of stability to accomplish anything, otherwise I could not function. I needed to create a concrete schedule of what should come first and then what should come next. I started this when I began high school. For example:

A.M.	5:00-6:00 practice accordion
	6:00-7:00 eat and shower
	7:00-3:00 school
P.M.	3:00-3:15 break
	3:15-4:15 homework
	4:15-4:30 dishes
	4:30-5:30 practice accordion
	5:30-6:00 eat
	6:00-6:15 dishes
	6:15-8:00 practice accordion

Still seeing myself in the mirror as if I were something out of a science fiction movie, I headed off to college fifteen hundred miles away when I was seventeen years old, in order to run away from this unknown entity I had become. I would call my parents, talk to my father, and sullenly say, "Dad, I am so very depressed, I do not know what is wrong with me?" He would answer back, "I will un-press you with an iron and your depression will disappear". Well, I really did not feel any support from his comment, especially since he chuckled as he said it.

By this time I was seeing the devil regularly, and I knew that both myself and the devil wanted me dead. When I spoke to my mother in my small apartment with a knife to my carotid artery, I explained frantically that this could be the last time that she would ever speak to me. Did my parents not understand that I was trying to escape my life through suicide? My brother called me and said, "Do not telephone mom anymore because your little suicide talk is making her upset." I went into such a deep dark hole that I did not come out for weeks. My brother is a good guy and he was just trying to protect our mother from my crazy talk.

Yes, at times I feel as though I am participating in the world, however, what kind of world is this. I am so confused and anxious. Seeing and hearing two or more things at once, especially hearing thunderous booms awaken me from my sleep, proves to be too many anxious moments for me. Praying and applying holy water to myself were two therapies that I used in order to remove the devil's torturous words and hallucinations. Also, practicing my accordion distracted me and kept my brain busy enough to concentrate on only one activity.

At twenty-two years old, I decided to move back home from college, hoping that things might be better. I started drinking excessively to escape my psychoses. Unfortunately, drinking gave me daily migraine pain. I started to waitress in order to make some money to buy a newer car. The empty void within me was unbearable. I felt as if I had the skeleton of a half person and half bug. When I moved back home, nothing had changed for the better. I remember saying chronically, "I just want to kill myself" in front of my parents, and they unfortunately decided that they would simply take me out for supper in order to placate me that evening. I immediately started crying a river in front of them; I believed that I had severe depression and no one seemed to take me seriously. As a result, no one reached out to hug, or even touch me at this vulnerable time in my life.

I felt as though my parents and brother were out to kill me. I would stay awake at night after I went to bed, and any little noise I heard scared me to death. I had horrific thoughts at night and I waited in my bed for all of them to come true. In the morning, when I opened my eyes after sleeping, I would see pictures of various objects rapidly flashing before my eyes; the objects flashed even if I had my eyes closed. These objects included knives dripping with blood, people with missing body parts, among other gruesome pictures. Most of the images flashed too quickly in order to be deciphered however. I could hear the noise whooshsh every time that I moved my eyes from side to side. I finally asked my mother if she would ever kill me, and she said no because she loved me more than anything else in this world. I know that I certainly did not feel that love my mother was supposedly giving to me. Maybe it had to do with my being adopted, maybe it was due to my schizophrenia, but I was sure in my mind that my father, mother and brother were certainly plotting to kill me.

Whenever I went into a store I felt anxious because of all of the people around me. Actually, I more specifically felt that I was in a wind tunnel, where everything was distorted. I could hear the wind circling around me and I could see a funnel-shaped white cloud also encircling me. Only being able to see close objects and not far into the funnel scared me. It felt as if I was looking through a pair of binoculars backwards. People also moved in blocks of space and came next to me very quickly.

For a few years, I had visual hallucinations of girls that were about forty feet tall. There were three of them, all wearing the same striped cotton dresses, but in different colors; one in green, one in purple and one in yellow. They were always located in the woods near my parent's home and I would speak with them. The only portion of my psychosis I did tell my parents was about the bothersome devil, which used to speak and appear before me on a regular basis. After my father passed away in 1993, I would see my dad regularly as a visual hallucination and I was also able to sense his spirit.

I suffered with daily migraines, which became worse after age twenty, so I made a neurology appointment hoping that the neurologist could lessen my pain. Unfortunately, I became addicted to the prescription narcotic given to me by the neurologist. The medication that the neurologist had prescribed for me contained a barbiturate component.

Before antipsychotics were discovered, barbiturates were given to patients with mental illnesses in order to control their psychoses. I truly believe that all of the barbiturates that I have taken over a ten-year span, did help to somewhat mask the seriousness and prevalence of my schizophrenia. Therefore, I was driven to go back to the neurologist with more frequency in order to obtain more medication, and as a result, the neurologist refused to give me any more of the narcotic because he could see that I was hopelessly addicted to it. I was beside myself, so I did the only rational thing in my sick mind; go to podiatry school so that I could write my own prescriptions as I needed them and relieve my own migraines. I knew that podiatrists wrote many prescriptions for pain relief because I spent a day with a podiatrist before I applied to podiatry school. So, I decided to go to podiatric medical school and I was pleased because I was sure that I was doing the right thing for myself. This made perfect sense to me at the time; because this guaranteed that I could write scripts for my painkiller when I needed it.

Before attending podiatric medical school, I met an angel, in 1991, who I would eventually marry. We met on a blind date. He was soft spoken, sweet, and full of old world Italian goodness and charm. Our love remains stronger than ever. My husband supported my idea to go back to school, but he never knew the reason why I was actually going back. In starting school, I was lucky to find a very good study companion and friend there because I had a very difficult time studying by myself. Three major reasons why I had trouble studying by myself were: sometimes I would understand the opposite of what the words actually stated in the books, I also had trouble remembering what I had just read and I had a hard time just focusing, period. My good friend and I would arrive at school early in the morning and she would discuss the salient points of what we would be tested on later. If only I could focus, I could listen in class, and absorb the material the first time that the professor taught it. I eventually made myself, through self-discipline and God's help, to focus on the professor's material in class. In May of 1998, I became Nicole Levesque, DPM.; I was thrilled.

CHAPTER 2
MY JOURNAL (1999-2000)

As soon as I passed my National Licensing Exam, I found myself filling out my own prescriptions immediately. This would have been definitely frowned upon by the medical community as a whole. I ended up taking so much narcotic medication because, I did not have the correct medication which I needed to heal what was truly ailing me. This was the reason why I had a psychotic breakdown in the middle of my second year surgical residency. Some schizophrenic people, try to hide their illness and stop their psychoses by taking alcohol, drugs or both of these substances. I took my fair share of prescription drugs also, in order to quiet my psychoses and escape my illness. However, if you remember, I chose a painkiller, which had an ingredient in it called a barbiturate. This painkiller helped me tremendously because it decreased the amount of pain I had as a result of my chronic migraines, and it also aided my schizophrenia because it controlled both my psychoses and anxiety to a certain extent. Schizophrenic people try to regulate their inner feelings, with something that will help them to relax and rid themselves of the chronic chaos in their minds.

* I am not feeling so well today. My mind, body, and spirit are desperately trying to keep up with the large volume of work during my surgical residency. I have many rotations such as: infectious diseases, internal medicine, vascular surgery, and of course my own specialty; foot and ankle surgery. I actually performed my first leg amputation today. Even though I felt excited while performing this surgery, I also felt somewhat melancholy for my patient. Thank God for the attending physicians, because they are always present in the surgical suite in order to aid the residents, who perform all surgeries, and guide us patiently towards the end of the surgical case.

* I am not pleased with myself because I am just taking too many painkillers for my body. I seem to have built up a tolerance to the pills I take for my migraines.

Although I feel dizzy, very rarely due to these pills cause dizziness, however today was one of those days I felt dizzy, since I did not eat lunch and I took extra medication on an empty stomach. A few of my colleagues commented on how thin I was getting; hopefully they do not suspect what is truly happening. It most certainly gives me great pleasure to care for my patients, and it is truly amazing how many different abnormalities of the foot and ankle there are.

* Taking at least twelve pills per day, I am actually swallowing twice the legal limit. I must stop, but I doubt I can quit

myself, because I suffer with debilitating migraines without those painkillers. I am stuck; I do not believe that I can decrease the amount of painkillers I take daily. Maybe if I take one less pill every week, my body will acclimate itself to this new schedule, and I will not have to go for help. I pray to Christ that he may hear my voice, because I can barely hear it myself, with all the noise going on in my head.

* Well it is two weeks later, and I reverted back to taking about twelve pills per day. These painkillers just seem to calm the voices in my head and make me feel placid in a high-stress arena, such as the hospital. God, it must be very painful for You to see one of your daughters act in such a reckless manner; I am so very sorry. I have tremendous guilt all of the time because I take more and more painkillers for my migraines. Please remove this burden from me Jesus.

* I made a delicious beef supper for my husband and myself tonight; however the communication between the two of us, is at best, strained. He is aware that I take too many pills daily, but he is unaware of how truly addicted I am. I do not have the fortitude nor the strength of heart to tell him just yet. He is my angel, and I do not want to make him anymore upset than I have to.

* Needing something comparable to the feeling I get when I am on my painkiller, I thought that maybe Valium would be a good substitute. I am aware that Valium could also be addictive, but certainly not as much as my painkiller (so I thought). My husband and I rented a videotape about Valium, helping

people who are very anxious, and they wish for that anxiety to go away. We also went on the internet and looked up an anxiety chat room. The people in the chat room were all talking about their medications, and how some were better than others. I still do not know what is truly wrong with me, so I hoped that Valium was indeed the replacement for my painkiller since it helped to quell my anxiety.

* God, I know that You are behind me all of the way, but I cannot feel or hear You. I know this is because I have caused a huge wall of disappointment to go up, brick by brick, due to my taking so many pills every day. We are both saddened greatly. I also take an anti-emetic, so that I can stop the feeling of vomiting up all of my pills during the day; so utterly glamorous Nicole. I am probably poisoning myself, but I cannot stop. My stomach is always in pain, so I am going to see a gastroenterologist; a physician my colleague recommended.

* Just coming back home from the gastroenterologist, I found him to be very pleasant and nonjudgmental. I told him that I was taking many antacids in order to stop the chronic pain in my stomach. The gastroenterologist ended up prescribing me a much stronger antacid, something called an H2 blocker, and booking me for an endoscope so that he could really see what was going on in my stomach. The following week, I am on the schedule for the test. The endoscope revealed three large ulcers: two gastric and one duodenal. No wonder that I am in pain! The gastroenterologist states that I was to continue the H2 blocker, and to come back for a check-up in one month.

* I also went to visit a new primary care doctor, hoping and praying that he would write me a prescription for my pervasive anxiety. The physician refused to write me for a tranquilizer such as Valium, however he did give me a prescription for more of my drug of choice, my painkiller. My heart was racing so fast and I had only eaten very sparsely for a week. As a result, I was dehydrated, and told to go to the emergency room for re-hydration.

* I must stop taking so much medication because I do not respect myself anymore and neither does my husband. I feel as though my heart will just stop one day and this is how I will die.

* I had a breakdown of some kind today; it is September of 1999. I had performed two surgeries the morning of the breakdown, and casually walked out of the hospital after I had finished my dictations. I drove home, remembering nothing else. I was still trying to mask my psychotic symptoms. I actually walked out of the hospital after I completed my two surgeries of the morning, and drove myself home, just as if nothing had happened. I left all my patients in the hospital without a physician, came home, and turned on the television. Not even realizing that I left the hospital, I sat on my couch and I could not remember what I was actually doing before I sat down at home. My attending physician called me at home and asked me, "What is the problem?" She told me to get right back to the hospital, otherwise my job would be in jeopardy. I nonchalantly stated that I was feeling tired and that I would not be coming back in today. Of course, I lost my job and my career within about fifteen minutes of being home. This was just fine with me because my brain could not process what had just happened. I called both my husband and mother, sometime after I had taken a nap, and told them rather bluntly that I had quit my job. Both of them said that they did not believe me, but they soon learned that this was the truth within the next couple of days. At this point, I am sure that the anxiety was responsible for me quitting my job and career, however, I never thought that this tragedy could have been due to another mental illness or been the fault of a psychotic breakdown.

* I do not know why, but I feel as though I am a step behind everyone else, however, my mind is going faster and faster. I also feel like isolating myself from others.

What could be wrong with me? I believe that I have an anxiety problem because my pulse races, I begin to sweat, and feel dizzy when I think of going outside. My poor husband, who would rather do things outside the apartment, makes concessions on the weekends and stays inside our apartment with me. We never do anything due to my isolationism. He has stuck by me like no one else would ever care to do. I feel so guilty, but I cannot help this chronic isolationism.

* My husband bought some books and tapes on how to cure my anxiety, if this is what I truly have. I read the books, listened to the tapes and tried to work the programs contained in both the books and tapes, but why was this not working?

Maybe I am destined to be isolated and always miserable. Maybe I do not have anxiety at all, but I have something else. My mother keeps pushing me to go see a psychiatrist, and I do not think that I need any help right now. I am sick of feeling so badly inside God; I seek Your guidance always, however, You seem to be so very silent. Please help me!

* All I do during the day are the dishes, laundry and cook, while the rest of the day is spent in front of the television staring at a program that I do not even care for. God, I beg of You, to please help me feel better. I am a shell of a human and cannot seem to become a true person; I feel so empty inside. What am I doing wrong? I love You; help me please. I am depressed and I cry all of the time. These actions and feelings are not of a normal person. My husband thinks that I should go to my primary care physician, so I have an appointment tomorrow. We will see what happens. I know that I cannot mention the voices I hear, or how my husband's face changes as if it were made out of play dough, the night terrors I experience, or that my soul goes out of my body too often to count. I am afraid that the doctor might place me in a mental institution if he finds out about all of my problems.

* I just came back from the primary care physician that I went to see, and he gave me an anxiolytic medication and very simply told me to go back to work at the hospital. When I arrived home, I felt so utterly vulnerable because he did not seem to appreciate that I could no longer function as a human being, never mind as a surgeon and physician. I was ready for another breakdown because I felt so very fragile. So as a result, my husband called a neurologist to see if he

could diagnose me properly. The neurologist did give me Xanax, which is a kind of antianxiety medication and best of all, he was compassionate toward my plight, which consisted of quitting my job and having a nervous breakdown. Unbelievably though, both doctors that I went to see, never mentioned that I should see a psychiatrist.

* I just cannot ever seem to go for a pleasant walk on a pretty day, in order to enjoy the beautiful scenery around me. This would do my soul so much good, but I can not go outside because I need to isolate myself, as if I were a hermit. I never cared for family functions, because I always had some sort of apprehension to attend them, and I do not know why. Maybe it was because I was not happy within myself, so I could not be happy with others either. Remembering that I always needed time for myself during the family function, I would hide myself in a room away from the other kids and adults in order to quiet my head down. I was always happiest when I was alone. I also got very tired quickly and needed a respite.

* Maybe acquiring some sort of structure in my life would make me feel better.

I need to read a certain amount per day, exercise a certain amount and eat properly with vegetables and fruits. Well, I tried but I cannot seem to focus on anything that I am doing at the moment. Maybe there is not enough blood flowing through my head? No, this cannot be the case, because the blood vessels dilate when I have my daily migraines, so that I have more than enough blood flowing through the vessels in my brain.

* Every day I wake up, I feel more nervous, and visibly shake at times. I am aware of the poem, "Footprints in the Sand" and that You, God are carrying me at this point when I have trouble doing anything for myself. However, please send me some relaxation and relief from my tension. I do not even breathe properly in the shower. I must run out of the shower after about eight to ten minutes, because I am not filling my lungs with air properly and I feel faint. I run to my bed and concentrate on my breathing. Once I get my breathing under control, I feel much less shaky.

* I feel desperate and selfish all at once, because I know that there are so many other people in this world of ours that are worse off than I am. However, I also feel like an empty shell of a person-bug, who does not have the ability to care for or love anyone at this juncture of my life. Maybe I am being punished for something I have done. I really wish that I could in good conscience commit suicide, but I cannot because I am Catholic.

God, in the bible it states that You will not give me anything that I cannot handle or endure. Well, I am on the brink between enduring and not enduring at all. There is a huge brick wall between You and me God, because of the painkillers I take and because I do not take the time to speak with You anymore. Living is my hell!

* I do not understand how my husband can go to work daily, face other people and be so confident about it. I guess I also used to do that, however it seems so utterly removed from my psyche that I cannot imagine it anymore. I cannot even walk out of my house these days. I am currently reading

another book on anxiety and panic attacks. It seems as though I could also be suffering from panic attacks because my husband and I decided to go to a restaurant and due to a panic attack, I had to leave quickly. My husband paid the bill and he asked for doggie-bags. I was only trying to please him by actually going out of the house, however it back-fired. He was angry with me, and said that unless I get some psychiatric help, he would never go out with me again. How could I blame him?

* Using four different pharmacies, I was taking about fourteen painkillers per day, and I did not want this to be traced back to me, because I know that this is the wrong way to do things. Using these different pharmacies soon became expensive. My mother sent me some money with good intentions and I used it for my painkillers; what a rotten daughter I am. Here my mother was trying to defray the cost of our rent or car insurance, but I was selfish and used the money for my painkiller. Nicole, you really need to get it together, and do something drastic about this addiction or you will end up in a grave sooner than later.

CHAPTER 3
REHABILITATION

We had lived in New York for quite a few years. I needed a fresh start geographically, away from the hospital that I used to work at. Also, my husband needed a shorter commute time, to and from work. I knew that the move would help me psychologically, and allow me not to be so anxious, because I was going to be physically away from where I had my psychotic break, which occurred in the hospital that I had worked in. When we were looking for a place to stay, every time I went to see an apartment which I liked, it happened to look totally different when I went to see it for a second time. I just could not explain this phenomenon; I was confused.

So, we finally made the move to Connecticut and I continued to write prescriptions for myself because I had a medical license in this state also. I certainly did not decrease the amount of painkillers I was taking when I got to Connecticut. I believe that the pharmacy next door to us, figured out that I was writing my own scripts, but no one in the pharmacy ever said anything to me. Sometimes the almighty dollar speaks quite loudly, and my painkiller happened to be expensive. In addition, this was a brand new pharmacy trying to stay afloat and the store obviously needed my business. After I would visit the pharmacy, my day basically consisted of watching television and taking naps on the couch. My husband did not like to hug me very much because my vertebral bones were protruding out of my back. At five feet, nine inches tall, and weighing just one hundred and twenty lbs., I was ugly and ashamed of myself.

Feeling awful inside myself most days, I was not usually in a good mood, however, I tried to be as positive as I could be. God, please help me feel better; if not for me, then please do it for my husband. He loves me so much and I cannot seem to show him the love that I have for him. My head is full of terror and violent thoughts constantly.

I try to fight it; sometimes it works and other times it does not. My husband is a very helpful and gentle man; he makes supper, does the dishes and washes and folds the laundry. I know that I should be doing these chores, but I do not care much at this point.

What a great husband I have because he is so very worried about me and my illness. He is always asking me to go to see another doctor for a correct diagnosis.

Would I be able to tell another doctor that I feel like an empty shell, or that I have a huge bug with an exoskeleton wrapped around my body? I most certainly could not tell the doctor that I see and hear things, or that I constantly go in and out of my body. I pray that all of this mayhem will eventually stop, and therefore I just do not think that seeing a physician at this time is the right choice for me. I am terribly depressed because I am caught between listening to my husband or listening to my own feelings. I have yet to see a psychiatrist though.

Why do I feel so safe around animals, but not so safe around people? I think it is because I feel threatened by people, in comparison to animals, who are ready to show me love at all times. Whether I am in a good mood or a bad mood, the animal loves me unconditionally. I love my two cats, and I do not know if I could make it daily without them.

I feel as though people look at me and it turns their stomachs, and then at other times I feel invisible to others. People are always speaking badly about me, especially at mass. Whenever I hear a whisper in church, I know that people are taking pot shots at me, and I am constantly turning around to see who is talking about me.

I am very nervous and anxious this morning, so I will do my exercises. I feel that I must isolate myself today, just like any other day. I think that I will walk to the nearest sandwich shop to order two sandwiches to go, so that I will not have to cook this evening. This is a dilemma, because I will spend at least one hour actually convincing myself that going outside is safe for me. God, please help me when I attempt to go outside. I just ended a conversation that my mother and I were having on the telephone and she seemed interested in coming up to visit us and I cannot wait. It would be so much fun to have someone here to talk to, but the only problem we have, is that she likes to shop and I like to isolate. I walked ten minutes on the treadmill and did ten sit-ups so far today. I promise to do the remainder of my exercise later on today.

I do not feel like watching television, so I am listening to my new compact disc called "Meditation." Why do I always think of suicide? I feel worthless and I want to kill myself. The perfect technique, of how I envision killing myself, is stabbing myself deeply with a butcher's knife, within my abdominal aorta, and allowing myself to bleed to death internally. I am ready to meet my maker at anytime.

I keep seeing a hallucination of some type of animal running from me, and I wish this hallucination would leave me alone because it frightens me. Maybe this hallucination occurs due to my nervousness and anxiety. I have not decreased the intake of my painkiller and I am disgusted with myself. I do not think that I could successfully get off of this medication without dying. Coming off of barbiturates is difficult medically speaking, due to possible brain seizures which can occur while decreasing the dosage of the barbiturate component of my painkiller. I would need to come off of my painkiller in some sort of a medical facility, where the doctors could watch my progress.

God, I truly believe that You are behind me and pushing me in the right paths of life. You are my ultimate advisor, and I just need to listen to You when it is silent. Your angels come to visit me at times, especially my two guardian angels; one rests on each of my shoulders. I also feel that there are other spirits in my house, and I wonder if they are good or bad spirits?

My mother is here, in our apartment, and she noticed that I am much too skinny because I do not eat properly. She seems aware of my medication problem, of writing my own prescriptions, however, she is not saying anything about it to me. I can see the worry in my mom's saddened brown eyes. I had a friend who just died from a drug overdose, which is so unbelievably overwhelming. I do not want to go that route, but to tell you the truth, I do not seem to care that much anymore. One day in February of 2001, I stumbled to the phone and opened the phone book to psychiatrists. I closed my eyes and I asked God passionately to please direct my finger to a psychiatrist who would not judge me because I took so many painkillers.

I made the phone call and as a result my psychiatrist's appointment was schedule for today. The psychiatrist stated that I must enter the rehabilitation center, which is in the psychiatric ward of my local hospital, in order to come off of the painkiller safely. The psychiatrist made all of the arrangements for me, so that I could enter the facility in just a few days. In two days, the center had a spot for me. My mother, husband and myself all went to register me at the hospital. Not thinking clearly, I had hidden pills in my socks and pockets for use in the rehab center. Obviously, I was not serious at the beginning of my treatment.

So, I took out a few pills to take immediately, and when my mother saw this, she grabbed all the rest of the pills quickly. She said to me that she could not believe that I was attempting to sneak my painkillers into the rehab facility. After a cursory physical exam, the chief psychiatrist gave me two large pills of barbiturates in order to start decreasing my addiction to the painkillers. Well, he did not calculate the dose quite right and as a result, the two large pills rendered me unconscious for six hours, and the staff strapped me to a wheelchair for those six hours so that I would not hurt myself.

After taking the loading dose given to me by the doctor, I woke up six hours later to people that I did not recognize, except for my mother and husband. I had forgotten what I was there for, when I first became conscious. These people were laughing loudly, some were crying and others still, were just there with confusion written all over their faces. My mother told me that my neck was hyper-flexed onto my chest for the six hours that I remained unconscious. The only thing I seem to recall from those six hours was my mom giving me a pillow to place under my chin, so that my neck would not hurt. I grabbed the pillow in my stupor, grateful for the comfort it gave me.

I was finally able to hold my head up on my own, however, I was so very confused; it was as if I woke up in the mirrors of horror at an amusement park. The nurses rushed down to me when I finally awoke, and gave me my own room in the psych ward. The nurses spoke to me briefly, but I was still not sure why I was there. I felt as if I had a lock on my frontal cortex which I called " brain freeze," because my forehead and frontal lobe felt as if they were frozen. I had to go along with anything that anyone said to me, because I had no choice in the matter; I was utterly confused. It felt very strange because I needed to be spoken to very slowly, so that I could understand. It must have been at least two hours before I realized that something was not quite right, and I asked my mother and husband what had happened to me? They explained about the loading dose of the barbiturate being too strong for me, and when I awoke, I had trouble forming thoughts, words and sentences. I could not remember where I was born, where I grew up or where I lived at the present time.

The nurses in the rehab center were superior; they were in and out of my room constantly checking in on me. No one judged me at the center just because I was a physician in a psychiatric ward. In fact, the staff was ultra-helpful to me. The staff made sure that all of my needs were met. I pretty much accepted everything which was being done to and for me because I was in the throws of becoming clean off of my painkiller, one day at a time. I absolutely had nothing left in me, because I had been taking various narcotics for approximately ten years. I had given myself up to an expert team of doctors and nurses, as well as aides, who collectively would eventually help me to leave this medication behind. My husband and mother stood by with tears in their eyes, while nurse after nurse tried to successfully draw blood from my body. I felt all dried out with nothing left to give. However the fourth nurse entered my room, and she drew the blood from my wrist. Well, that was both very painful but joyous when I saw blood coming through the syringe. One obstacle bravely faced and finally conquered. I wanted to be as positive as I could be.

I had a 9:00 meeting with the chief psychiatrist, who actually runs the inpatient psychiatric ward program I was attending. After many questions and answers, back and forth, the psychiatrist finally left my room. There were two wings in the rehab center and I was on the wing which was the more restrictive of the two. After not sleeping a wink all night long, I got up and was still very confused on my second day. I asked one of the nurses that had been in the psych ward for a long time, if I should be having this much trouble answering questions, and doing simple tasks. The nurse answered me, and stated that all people react differently to the loading dose and it's effects. I noticed that I was seeing and hearing more things than usual also.

My husband and mother were there with me every step of the way, as long as the visiting hours were in effect. I awoke the very next morning to find that I did not know what to do with the thermometer that was given to me in order to take my temperature.

The nurse's aide waited to see if I could figure out what to do with the thermometer, but I could not. I also could not successfully convey what I needed or wanted because I had what I called, "brain freeze". This felt as if my brain was actually frozen and had a giant pad lock on it, so that no information could travel in or out. I was not speaking properly at this time, and it sounded just like gibberish. So, thinking that they were doing me a favor, my mother and husband would finish my sentences for me. This was the first problem that I had with both of them, because how was I supposed to learn how to speak properly again, unless I practiced with them and others?

My mother is a very strong-minded person and I knew that I needed to stick up for my rights, which I had never done before. At times, she treated me as if I were a five year old. My husband and mother would talk about me in my room, at the rehab facility amongst themselves, as if I were invisible. They did not mean any harm, however, my self-esteem plummeted even further. I explained to them, one at a time, that if I were going to get better, there would have to be some changes made, and one particularly important change was that when I spoke up for myself, they should take the time to listen to me and not to quickly discount what I say. I knew that I had two very strong, opinionated people in my life, who loved me very much, and so I had better take matters into my own hands and become strong like they were in order to be part of the conversation.

Since I was very shy about coming out of my room and mingling with other patients, I remained in my room as much as I could. My husband and mother finally coached me to come out of my room on the third day. I was terrified, but I met a couple of nice people in the large community room, although there was a young lady in the community room with uncontrolled bipolar illness. The atmosphere there felt circus-like, where everyone had different affects and illnesses, and they all seemed to be performing for the staff. There are many mentally sick patients in the psychiatric ward, however, I met two especially nice friends; one was suicidal and the other was bipolar. They always checked on me every night before I went to bed. They seemed genuinely concerned about me.

I was not eating much, except a few crackers per day, but peeling an orange at 10:00 pm seemed like a good idea. This orange was the first true food that I had eaten while I was sober. Well, I was proud, however, by 1:00 am when the med-nurse was passing the medications out, as she came through my door, I vomited all over her. She said to me that by the look of things, she would definitely have to baby-sit me tonight as she left the room to clean herself. I guess the old adage is true; that an orange is gold in the morning but lead at night.

Eventually, that same nurse and I became very good acquaintances and I looked forward to her coming onto her shift. She always had an interesting story to tell me at whatever time she came in on duty. Unfortunately, I could not sleep for the first five days I spent in the institution because I was anxious. I was anxious because there would always be someone, who came around to the various rooms at night with a flashlight, in order to see if the patients were either sleeping or awake. During those first five days, I had the worst hallucinations I had ever experienced; I had actually been to hell and back. These hallucinations were so real and guttural that they came from the devil himself. I saw the devil in every hallucination and no matter how hard I tried, I could not access God.

Hearing all kinds of bug noises and snakes hissing, I cried because the noises came from the core of the earth and arose straight to me; how utterly sickening. This occurred for the first five nights I was in detoxification.

During the day, many doctors and nurses would come into my room in order to ask me various questions. When the chief psychiatrist on the psychiatric ward heard, via the other doctors, how real and disturbing my hallucinations were, he immediately placed me on one thousand milligrams of Depakote, which helped me somewhat. The remainder of my hallucinations were minor in comparison to the hallucinations I experienced before taking the Depakote.

I began coming out of my room more and more, because I found my two friends were also out in the large community room. One Saturday, my friend and I watched one TV channel all day long. It was my best day there because I needed something uncomplicated to watch, and the ability to drift off when I needed to. I felt relaxed and wonderful. My mother was very supportive of me because she was always there for the visiting hours and sometimes she managed to stay even when the visiting hours were actually over.

The staff grew very tired of this extra time that she spent with me, and she in turn had to abide by the rules. At least my mom tried, and I thanked her for that.

I was not eating anything except for crackers and ginger ale. The physician on call placed me on intravenous fluid, since I was losing weight and also dehydrated due to low consumption of fluids. I could not afford to lose any more weight since I was five feet, nine inches tall and weighed only one hundred and ten pounds. However the staff turned off the intravenous machine approximately forty-eight hours after it started. My mother was constantly bringing in food from the outside, trying desperately to entice me to eat anything. My husband would always have some soda in his hands and ask me to drink every few minutes. This was so tiresome, however it helped to keep me alive.

Obviously, I looked better in a couple of days because the staff moved me from one wing, to the other less restrictive wing. This was exciting to me because it meant that I was getting better. There was one very special staff member who was neither a doctor nor a nurse, but he used to give me pep talks. He would tell me how genuine of a person I was, and how seriously I took my recovery. I still remember him to this day, and thank him for all of the meaningful talks we had in my room.

The nurse that had become my friend, the one I unfortunately threw up on, confided in me that she had her own problems with addiction. I was shocked, however, I wished her luck on her own fight with the painkiller she was struggling with. Sadly, I knew that quitting that particular painkiller was impossible to do on one's own, because she had taken her drug of choice for a long time, just like I had.

Her situation made me realize how prevalent and pervasive drugs are in the community. I have a friend in the same predicament but with alcohol instead of drugs. He has been fighting this problem for a very long time. Sometimes I think that a person addicted to alcohol might be in a worse situation, since alcohol is so easily accessible. It is true when others say that drug addicts and alcoholics are people you will find in all of the socio-economic strata within society, and that drug addiction and alcoholism are truly medical illnesses.

I wrote my husband a short letter so that he could have something of me at home, while I am in this facility. Here it is:

Dearest Husband,

How I ache for the day that we can be together again. I know that I will conquer this disease that has infected my body, for approximately ten years. I am having so many strange thoughts; also I am both seeing and hearing things. I have not slept in four nights but this is alright. I will continue to be as positive as I can be. Currently, I am sitting with a friend in the larger community room. She asked about you and I told her that you had to go back to work today. Sweetheart, please hope and pray for my recovery. I miss you and love you. I looked out of my window for mom at 7:00 am and I have not seen her yet, as we had planned to do last night.

Love Always,
Nicole

I had some letters that I wrote to my mother, but unfortunately I misplaced them. Writing in my journal, or writing to someone, was the first task that I completed in the morning. Writing gave me a sense of peace and it also made me feel as though the person I was writing to or about at that moment was with me. I missed my mother and husband all day long, but thank God when the visiting hours came; I was elated. Both of them brought me freshly washed clothes, and bought me little presents from the gift shop downstairs. What a wonderful, thoughtful family I have. I appreciate them so much, but it was hard to show them the appreciation since I had a flat affect most of my days at the rehab center.

I made my bed sober for the first time in ten years; wow did that ever feel good. The bed was made up okay, but it will be better next time. Where I sit and look outside, I can see a brick wall with pigeons flying back and forth. This scenery is not exactly conducive to acquiring a sound state of mind. However, I made a friend, who seemed always in a good mood, and she asked me if I wanted to do some art with her. I said, "That would be great," and we started to color; how fun. She let me borrow a popular magazine, and that was also wonderful to read, since all I had were my religious books in the room. Also, my mother brought me the "Reader's Digest", which I read from cover to cover.

I was taking my addiction very seriously and I told myself every day, that I would never again pick up my drug of choice and take it. I would have been so embarrassed to have been put right back into this rehabilitation center because of non-compliance when I went back home. The wall between God and myself was finally down. I could pray to Him and feel Him; especially with the answers that He gave me. He was finally listening to me. I was the only person on the psychiatric floor, who was getting sober at this time, however, all of the other patients struggled to keep themselves sober, because they all had taken drugs and alcohol to excess before. The other people on the floor were mostly bipolar, schizophrenic or epileptic.

My brother called me on the psychiatric unit from his home in Massachusetts, twice. That was so very thoughtful of him as he made me laugh and feel special just because he had taken the time to call me. This pumped some self-confidence in my veins, and I felt as though I were walking on a cloud. My brother is a very special man, because he is very sweet to me, but yet has a solid manly exterior. He has two beautiful daughters and they also talked to me on the phone. This meant so much. There was a nurse, who came into my room today, and I thought that we were just speaking as friends, but how naïve I was. The nurse ended up writing everything down that I said and I really learned a lesson about watching out what I say to other people.

I need to write down what it is I wish to tell my husband and mother, because it seems as though that they still never give me a chance to talk. Maybe if I wrote something meaningful and read it to them out loud, this would show them how serious I am about this subject. I hope no one gets offended. If they both love me, like they say they do, both of them will not become resentful, but instead, they will understand that I will be doing what is best for my recovery.

Here is what I decided to write to both my husband and mother:

I do not mean to be rude, or to look as if I do not care when you visit me, however, sometimes I block certain situations out of my mind, which are too painful to even think about. For example, you might have noticed that I do not ask about my cats, because it is just too painful. I wait for you all day long, and I think the world of you both. Please give me a chance to talk while both of you listen to me. I hope that you do not take offense and judge me, but I feel that being here together is so important that it literally means everything to me. This addiction hit me hard, both physically and mentally, but I try not to dwell on that. I think that I have learned to cover my feelings and thoughts over with laughter.

Even though laughter is good for you, keeping a journal and reflecting upon your true feelings is better. I do need more help. Today is the second day that I made my bed sober, and the bed came out much better than before, because I took pride in doing it.

This may seem like a small task to you, however, I have not taken pride in anything for a long period of time. I am having such a difficult time remembering how to speak, write and do certain tasks. What is going on? I am looking forward to a full recovery, but for now, I have this moment in time.

Love Always,
Nicole

Both my husband and mother appreciated the letter that I had written to them. Since that time, I have been able to speak freely to both of them, and that is a huge victory for me. My mother is the one who egged me on to keep this diary, and I am so grateful to her, because it feels wonderful to review what happened to me before and after I went into the psychiatric ward. The staff and the other patients were so pleasant to me, because I isolated myself quite a bit and they were rooting for me to leave my room and get better. There was a rule that no one was ever allowed to go into another patient's room, however, sometimes my friend and I broke that rule so that she could visit me when I was isolating myself. Isolationism is a sign of schizophrenia, which I later learned. In the rehab center, the weekends were more lackadaisical since we were allowed to sleep in until 8:00 am instead of 7:00 am, Monday through Friday. All of the patients would form a line prior to breakfast in order to have our vitals checked. This was a very important, yet standard procedure at the rehabilitation center. I never ate breakfast, lunch or dinner with the other patients, and so I would basically go without eating. I just wanted to be in my own little room, by myself.

Taking pride in things that I had accomplished was my usual modes operandi when I was younger. Then approximately ten years ago, I stopped caring about what I did and how I did it. Lately, within the last week, I could start feeling some semblance of that pride again; this felt wonderful. My mother was very impressed with my letter and the happiness I fostered inside of myself, but I was not quite sure how my husband had received it. I know that my husband wanted me sober, and expressing no more lies. He wanted me just like I was before I started taking the painkiller. Yes, I feel differently inside since I entered the psychiatric ward, as the painkiller was slowly leaving my body. Well, my husband and I would just have to learn how to talk like other couples do, and decide things together. We were used to my husband making most of the decisions and me agreeing to them. I actually had an opinion about certain things now, because I was clean. The painkiller, these last ten years, rendered me unable to speak openly, because there was a wall built up between my husband and I. This was going to take time, however, I was willing to be patient. My husband was from the "old school", but I was sure that I could get him to speak with me at home. This wall of mistrust and unhappiness had to come down, brick by brick.

I was feeling so well inside, therefore I started eating with the other patients and having two Boost drinks per day. We even watched my favorite show, Survivor, on television with everyone else; what a fun night. Lately, everything is starting to look great; I hope that I always feel this well. No migraines, no aches and pains in my stomach or anywhere else; I just feel first-rate. I feel so good, especially because I had read this letter to my husband and that, in turn, removed the stress of having to express myself, without forethought or preparation. Thank you God for allowing the reading and discussion of that letter to happen peacefully. I was ready to go home (in my own mind). Although, I could feel that my turn was coming up to be discharged, I was both jubilant yet sad, for I would not see these people in the psychiatric ward, who became my friends and acquaintances, any longer.

I was working diligently on having a stronger will, so that I could even come out daily into the large community room to converse with the other patients. The interaction with others was amazing to me, since I could not even attempt to come out of my little room just about two weeks ago. I was always anxiety-filled and very interested when all of the patients would gather to find out who was to be discharged that day. The staff was still collecting blood work on me after about two weeks into the program and I am positive it was to make sure that I remained clean, which I did. I took this very seriously.

Every day I would ask the doctors and nurses if I should be feeling a certain way, or if I was developing properly without taking the painkiller daily? The answer would always be, that all people respond differently to the rehab process. So, I knew that I was not doing wonderfully, however, I was probably doing adequately. I was definitely diagnosed with something other than addiction, because I was still on Depakote. My hallucinations were a bit better due to the Depakote, however, that medication did not make me feel like myself.

Inside my head was so full of terrible thoughts. I was afraid that I would act upon one of those thoughts, and that the police would leave me in the psychiatric ward forever; please God, do not allow this to happen to me. I still was seeing and hearing things and so the chief psychiatrist asked me if I felt as though I was medicated when I took the Depakote. I told him yes. Very sadly I had thoughts of both suicide and homicide. Everyone knows how much I love my two cats, and unfortunately I had thoughts of me skinning them alive. This is only one of those terrible thoughts that

I had to live with. My voices expressed themselves very quietly. So, I would communicate with them and tell them that they must speak louder so that I could understand them. Truly believing that I could possibly have schizophrenia, I decided not to relay all of my symptoms to the doctors or chief psychiatrist.

My mother was always at the hospital at 7:00 am, even though we could not see each other until 2:00 pm to 4:00 pm. This occurred because there were rehabilitation classes for me to attend to during those times. I went to an art class, relaxation class, dual diagnosis class, and usually the doctor would visit me between classes. I was upset early on because my mother could not visit with me when I needed her to, but I would have missed out on some very important dual-diagnosis classes at that time, if I would have spent all of my time with my mother.

The social worker tried to sign me up for another inpatient program. All of the doctors collectively did not think fifteen days of an inpatient program was enough for me to remain sober on the outside. Unfortunately, my insurance failed me and as a result, the social worker made an appointment for an outpatient program. "This was better than nothing," I thought to myself. Although, I was ready to go to another inpatient facility, I have to admit the truth in that I was so glad to be going home, finally. This news felt wonderful. I thought that my addiction would continue to get better ; in other words, that I would never crave my drug of choice again, after everything I had been through. The day finally came when they called my name for discharge. I was both excited, yet nervous because I would soon be alone with my addiction. I did not know or realize that I was going to crave my drug of choice as soon as I left the hospital. My husband thought that he had hidden all of my prescription pads, however, I had some stored away before I had left for the psychiatric ward.

It was so wonderful to smell the outside air after being released. It was early March now.

I am so sad due to how commercial medicine has turned out. I really needed another inpatient program and now my insurance company refuses to pay for it. It is abominable how the value of a human life, in a throwaway society, has become so utterly insignificant. I was given a case manager, who I got exactly one call from, in order to see how I was doing. I cannot forget to call the psychiatrist who placed me in the psychiatric ward to begin with. Unfortunately, I have many symptoms besides my addiction problem, but I do not know if I should express the truth to this psychiatrist, because I do not know him well enough yet.

CHAPTER 4
PSYCHIATRIST AND MEDICATIONS

It was March 2001, and I assumed that my hell had finally ended, when I completed detoxification during my stay in the psychiatric ward. However, unbelievably, my hell had just actually begun. I came home to a dirty apartment, where many flashbacks of taking my painkiller were running rampant through my mind. This bothered me, because I heard a voice in my head that stated that I should seek out some of my painkillers to ingest immediately, because I needed them, and I had not taken my painkillers for weeks now. Resisting temptation for only approximately three days after leaving rehab, I felt as though I could not wait any longer to get my hands on my narcotic. Again, I experienced the same rush from filling out my own prescription, and picking up the painkiller as I did before I entered detoxification. I was confused, because I had done all of that work in the psychiatric ward, so that I would never feel the urge to order my painkiller ever again. What just happened?

Well, after I swallowed some of my narcotic, the pills calmed me down greatly. Unfortunately, I was not proud of myself, but if my psychiatrist would not give me what I needed for my migraines and anxiety (to a lesser extent), I would have to take steps in order to quell my own problems. Believe me, this is not what I had planned for myself in coming home; what a fiasco. I cannot believe that I am currently writing in my journal, that I took my painkillers so soon after I was released from rehabilitation. I took the painkillers until all of the medication was gone. How disappointing and just plain stupid I was. However, I never wrote another prescription for my narcotic again, but I guess I had to try it just one more time. Some people self-medicate in order to partially drown out their psychoses and strange thinking patterns. Sometimes it works, and other times it does not.

I start my out-patient therapy program tomorrow and it is supposed to last approximately two weeks. Honesty is extremely important, so when I go tomorrow, I must own up to the fact that I was addicted to narcotics for ten years. I would like to make this point very clear once again; the reason I was addicted to my painkiller for so long, was that it used to control some of my anxiety, manage my migraines, and protect me from some of my psychoses, all at the same time. Being off of the painkiller, I would very noticeably tremble, due to my anxiety. Brighter days should be around the corner though. I hope that there is a psychiatrist at the out-patient program, who can dispense medications for what is actually wrong with me. Otherwise, I will call Dr.

Sloan, the psychiatrist, who placed me in the rehabilitation program in the first place, and he can diagnose me and set up a proper medication regimen for me. I think that I might have anxiety and a few other problems.

I cannot believe that this next set of events happened, however, I had a flat tire on the Merritt Parkway, so I did not make it to my first out-patient class. I called my husband, he left work in order to come and pick me up, while I sat at a Mobil station for four hours awaiting him. I did some thinking while I was at the Mobil station, and there was no reason why I could not take care of this problem myself. Why did I have to wait for my husband in order to have a flat tire fixed? So, I called the closest garage to me at the time, and asked for a tow truck to come and pick up my car, in order to expedite matters, for when my husband did indeed show up. If I had been on my painkillers, none of this problem would have been dealt with before my husband arrived. I realized at that moment, that my mind, and therefore my thoughts, were slowly coming back to me, and I was sincerely pleased. Thinking more clearly, I was able to have my car serviced by the time that my husband came to pick me up. My husband was very pleased with me, in that I was able to fix the problem on my own, instead of relying on him all of the time.

Today is the first day of spring; what a great day. I had my first out-patient meeting. With a minimal anxiety level, I actually reached out to others. God is to thank for this. Every day seems to bring me a step closer to my inner healing. What actually helps me is that, when I have an uncomfortable feeling around other people, I try to take my mind off of that feeling, and always remember that these feelings will eventually end. I must focus on the positive, because God made me strong so that I could rise up out of the negativity and go towards the light. I must remember that everyone has a soul, and the soul is good, therefore it just feels so wonderful to reach out and connect with people, at the outpatient clinic, even though these particular people are neurologically and psychiatrically stricken with mental illnesses.

My mind is playing tricks on me today. My addiction demon is teasing me to take some of my painkillers. It is almost impossible for me to stop myself from walking across the street, and picking up my prescription at the local pharmacy. God, please be with me today, because this way of thinking is self-deprecating. By writing in my journal, it helps to keep me focused, and feel as if there is a weight being lifted off of my shoulders; so much so, that I did not choose to pick up any painkillers at the local pharmacy today. I am doing laundry and cleaning my apartment, in order to use both distractive and self-soothing techniques. These techniques help the uneasiness that I am feeling today; I learned these techniques at the out- patient clinic.

I really and truly believe that I suffer from some sort of generalized anxiety.

Before benzodiazepines were in the arsenal of the physicians, barbiturates also helped to decrease some of the patient's anxiety and psychoses. The class benzodiazepines included such drugs as Valium and Xanax. I know that since I am not on barbiturates any more (through my painkiller), what I need is an anxiolytic medication, because I am miserable and I actually do not feel good inside of my own skin. I shake as if I have had ten cups of coffee, but the reason that my doctors do not want to give me the anxiolytic is because tranquilizers are addictive. Yes, I agree with them that tranquilizers are addictive, however, if I asked my husband to be in charge of how many pills I take during the day, this problem would be solved. I could also do this with my painkiller. My husband could be in charge of this medication, and I would only get one pill for every roaring migraine headache that I happen to suffer from.

I always realized both consciously and subconsciously, that there was something not quite right with me. I did not act as if I were a "normal" person. I had a panic attack at the restaurant my husband and I went to, so I ran out of the restaurant and my husband got the food to go. Now I am sure that I have some sort of psychiatric deficiency. At this point, I have gone to see my psychiatrist (the doctor that placed me in the psych ward) for two weeks, and we started on a medication regimen which included Zoloft and something to help me sleep at night because I am an insomniac. The antidepressant Zoloft was not working for me at all and certainly not for my panic attacks, nor my anxiety. This anxiety is an intense feeling, and I cannot even cope with my daily chores anymore. I have shortness of breath, chest pains, shaking all over, sweating from my palms, a migraine and it feels as though my heart is pounding out of my chest, besides the psychotic episodes that I suffer from. I have these symptoms, it seems, for no reason at all. I still suffer from seeing things which are not really there, hearing sounds which scare me, and smelling things which do not make sense. For example, I see the devil and ugly monsters, I hear a bomb go off in my head, usually when I wake up, and smell human remains in our walls at home. As you know, I also suffer from night terrors regularly. I was afraid to divulge all of my hallucinations to my psychiatrist, for fear of being placed back into the psychiatric ward of the local hospital.

God is watching over me; I am sure of that. I went to my primary care physician and he could not find anything wrong with me. Maybe these symptoms are all in my mind; I feel as though I am going crazy bonkers. I have had migraine headaches since I was a teenager, and stomach ulcers since I was in my early twenties. Going back to my psychiatrist, he replaced Zoloft with another antidepressant, which come to find out, did not work either. What could be wrong with me?

I have been extremely erratic this weekend and I know that I must be sick in the head. I confronted my mother about my sickness which I had all of my life, including the voices I hear, the hallucinations I see, and the wretched material I smell at times. My mother stated that she thought that I was very sick, and to tell my psychiatrist about this. I was still afraid that the psychiatrist would put me back in the psychiatric ward, so I decided not to tell him yet.

Thank God that my husband has the week off starting tomorrow because I miss him so much when he is at work. I thought about working myself, however, I do not think that I could, due to my panic attacks, anxiety, etc. I need to take baby steps in order to get better first. I am still having many horrific thoughts and I cannot seem to control them. Maybe God is punishing me for something that I did incorrectly. I am presently watching a show that I watched during my stay at the inpatient facility. This is good, because it arouses all of the pain and struggle I had gone through in the psychiatric ward, and reminds me never to go down that alley again. Goal for tomorrow: be myself, go out for a walk, call NAMI, go to Dr. Sloan's appointment, so that I may open up to him a bit more. I went to see my neurologist and he placed me back on my painkiller, but at a very small dosage. My husband has been doling the painkiller out ever since, and this has been working out wonderfully for my migraines.

Dr. Sloan was impressed that I stood up for myself, because I actually called him from my mom's home in Rhode Island on a Sunday morning, in order to beg him for an anxiolytic (benzodiazepine). He promised me that he would give me the benzodiazepine, when I came in on Tuesday. Thank You God. I could barely move and as a result, I just laid down for a couple of days waiting until my appointment with Dr. Sloan occurred. I learned that my feelings are important, and should definitely come first, especially if I am struggling this much in pain. Dr. Sloan told me that it was my job to take care of my feelings. Also, no more apologizing for my one relapse, because I expect to keep moving forward and making things better for myself.

This is it. This is the time that I am ready to open up to Dr. Sloan. I finally stated that sometimes I may see things and asked him if that would be " normal" or not?

He prodded me with questions and I answered all of them truthfully. One to two months later, he diagnosed me with paranoid schizophrenia. He asked me about my childhood, odd behaviors, if I hear things, and if I had discussed this with anyone. I said, "yes to everything." Dr. Sloan stated that I should tell my immediate family what my diagnosis is, and then read about schizophrenia as much as I could, in order to know the basics about the illness. I could not even say the word schizophrenia out loud, because it hurt too much psychologically, so my husband, mother, and myself called it the " S" word for a long time.

The psychiatrist started me on an antipsychotic regimen immediately. In fact, my first antipsychotic was Zyprexa. I took two doses of Zyprexa, and I actually felt, for the first time, like a human being. No more bug-like feeling, and when I looked in a mirror, I had two eyes, a nose and a mouth; I actually looked like everyone else, what a relief. I could also go outside, drive to the store and manage to get a haircut all in one day. Wow, I am so genuinely happy. Within the next few weeks, I had both good and bad days on the Zyprexa. Within the next few months however, I had bad side effects starting to occur. I started with akathisia for one, which is uncontrollable movements in the legs mainly, and sometimes even in other body parts. The devil was back also. For example, my husband and I went for a relaxing walk in the park. However, I saw everything in the park black and oily looking, with the devil's voice coming through the sky. Starting to see more hallucinations of that type, I was taken off of the Zyprexa.

The next antipsychotic which I was placed on was called Risperdal, but I had to come off of the Zyprexa first, which is the hardest part of changing medications, because of the withdrawal feelings that the medications give you. For me, Risperdal only lasted for two weeks, because my body, especially my head and neck, tightened up on me. Dr. Sloan did not like the looks of that side effect, so

I was immediately told to discontinue the Risperdal. Also, Risperdal was not helping my hallucinations either. When you finally find the antipsychotic that works for you, you will know it because basically you will not suffer from hardly any side effects, if any at all, and you will feel natural, as if you are not on any medication. As a result of the side effects of Risperdal, I left the psychiatrist's office with an antipsychotic called Geodon.

Geodon was a newer antipsychotic, so I had high hopes for it. Unfortunately, this medication ended up giving me too many side effects, such as: dry mouth, raised heart rate, and akathisia. The Geodon also never gave me true relief from my paranoid schizophrenia. I tried to stop the movements, caused by akathisia, by closing my eyes, praying and concentrating on stopping the movement of my body parts, but this was difficult. I knew someone else who was on Geodon, and it made him act out angrily. I wanted to have less chaos in my life. I would do anything to try and keep the antipsychotic I was on, so that I would not have to switch antipsychotics again, which always made me feel uncomfortable and strange inside myself. Unfortunately, here we go again. As a result of the akathisia, I was taken off of the Geodon slowly and started on another antipsychotic called Seroquel.

Seroquel seemed to be a good antipsychotic at the beginning, although I must admit that all of these medications are starting to blend together. When Dr. Sloan placed me on a higher dose of Seroquel, this also gave me akathisia and was basically not taming my bad thoughts nor my hallucinations. In all of the cases concerning my antipsychotics, I have always needed upper end dosing due to my hallucinations and night terrors.

However, this is when the akathisia would settle into my body. Also, my psychiatrist did not especially like Seroquel, for the simple fact that it had too large of a dosing range.

During this specific time, I decided to place everything in God's hands because I felt utterly discouraged and totally detached and dislocated from reality. This feeling used to happen to me quite a bit and as a result, I just could not get my soul and spirit back into my body. The next antipsychotic on the list to try was called Clozaril.

Clozaril is a medication that one must go to the hospital to give blood work every week for the first six months, and then every two weeks for the remainder of the time that the patient remains on Clozaril. Besides decreasing my metabolism to a crawl, this medication can actually decrease my white blood cell count. White blood cells are very important because they are our defense mechanism against sicknesses of all kinds. Also, Clozaril makes us hungry and gain too much weight. I gained forty pounds on Clozaril, and thirty-five pounds on all of the other antipsychotics combined. So far, all of these medications have managed to steal my personality, who and what I am inside, and make me feel as though I am outside of my body even more so than usual. Two other side effects were excessive sleepiness and increased salivation. I would really like to get on Vistaril, so that I can manage my weight more successfully, however, Dr. Sloan had other ideas. Obviously, again this was not my antipsychotic, and so I got off of the Clozaril slowly. I left Dr. Sloan's office with a brand new antipsychotic called Abilify.

I have been on the Abilify for approximately five months; and even though I still experience hallucinations and night terrors, the Abilify does not take away who I am, and what I am inside. It actually makes me feel good and I see the world through different eyes lately. I am hoping that the Abilify takes away all of my hallucinations of every kind, the longer that I remain on this medication. It seems as though, from my experience, that the longer I remain on my antipsychotic medication, the better that it works for me in terms of my behavior and having less hallucinations. I do not know the mechanism of this medication in my brain, however, this is not what is important. The results are what I care about most. Fortunately, this is most definitely the antipsychotic for me, because I no longer feel like an empty shell, or a huge bug-like creature inside and outside. Abilify is not perfect, however, it is the best of the antipsychotics for me out there now. Abilify is Dr. Sloan's drug of choice for my schizophrenia, however, all of the other antipsychotic medications that I spoke about, can be very successful in other people.

My husband asked the psychiatrist about my going on disability. Dr. Sloan stated that he thought that this would be a good idea. I received my disability within approximately one year of applying for it. Also, I was told that it would be retroactive from the time I had my psychotic break down, during my work at the hospital in 1999.

Every once in a while people are re-assessed as to whether they can keep their disability benefit or not. It is not much money, but it helps out the household and that makes me feel satisfied. I feel as though that I actually deserve the money, which I collect each month.

The next few paragraphs speak about supportive medications to the antipsychotics and how they help our illness. Unfortunately, I have been having trouble sleeping at night, which I communicated to my psychiatrist. He in turn gave me Ambien, which helped me to sleep about four hours per night. I felt better and more refreshed.

Since I have been up all of these nights, I learned to meditate and also perform deep breathing exercises. Actually, I believe that the night terrors were keeping me up along with some auditory hallucinations. People have conversations in my ears and I cannot seem to stop them. Sometimes the conversations are loud, and at other times they are soft. When they are soft, I ask the voices to speak a little louder so that I may understand them. However, Dr. Sloan told me never to pay attention to any of my voices, because this is giving the voices importance and time out of my life in order for me to listen to something which is not real.

My husband and I are just back from my cousin's wedding, and I cannot express to you how much my Xanax helped me to be able to mingle with the other guests and remain centered within myself. I was still slightly nervous, however, I felt cool, calm and collected because I mostly felt relaxed in a room full of family and strangers. Now, all the while Dr. Sloan is changing my antipsychotic, he is also tweaking my supportive medications. For example, my antidepressant changed from Zoloft to Paxil to Wellbutrin and finally to Effexor. The best part of it all, was that I was not thinking of suicide as much anymore on Effexor. I thought that if I could feel this good, why would I ever consider taking my own life?

My psychiatrist added Cogentin to my cocktail of medications, because it eased my akathisia. Today, I was able to go outside without feeling too much nervousness and went for a power walk. I also lifted weights, stretched out, finished two loads of laundry, changed the bed linen and brought the trash out. God, thank You for Your wonderful guidance and all encompassing love. I feel You so deeply in my heart, my soul and my mind. This is the day that I totally turn my life over to You. I am no longer in control. I have felt great for the past three days, and I know that this is because of You, my higher power.

Topomax is a mood stabilizer and it is given to me primarily for my migraines; my neurologist gives this to me. Sometimes I need two hours of naptime and there is nothing wrong with that, because my entire medication profile makes me sleepy. Most of our brains are actually hard-wired differently than the non-schizophrenic brain. I know that I often feel very energetic but confused and the medication profile that I take daily actually helps this phenomenon. This is what I have experienced for many years; confusion.

Xanax is my antianxiety (anxiolytic) medication and I am still having some problems sleeping. I would like to increase my Xanax ER at bedtime, however when I approached Dr. Sloan with the idea, he stated that he would keep me on the three milligrams per day and not increase the Xanax at all. The nature of Xanax is such that, if I would have taken six milligrams per day, my body would have acclimated itself to it. As a result, six milligrams daily would not work any better than three milligrams daily. Therefore, there was no reason to increase the amount of my Xanax.

I always enjoyed writing my goals in my journal for each specific day. Here is an example of this.

My goals for today are:

Say my prayers
Do laundry
Clean the pantry
Only drink water
Calm down
Do not get so depressed
Listen to the "Meditation" CD

God, I feel as though I should be a better person. I need to read the Bible more, and not just repeat the same prayers over and over. I need to talk to You God because You are my savior. Please use all of my breaths as prayers for those less fortunate than myself, and my situation. I also should remember my two guardian angels everyday, and speak to them because, they are here specifically in order to watch out for me. God, I ask You to give me purity of heart, purity of mind, and purity of soul. Please watch over me most powerful Jesus; You are the light of the world.

I do not want to isolate myself so much, but since I was a little girl, I have always felt the urgency to isolate. I feel so safe and happy in my apartment, where no one can hurt me and I cannot hurt anyone else in turn. During the weekends, I really have to work hard in order to be able to go out with my husband. At least I am not completely house bound anymore. At the moment, I am not able to even get the mail or to take out the trash during the week days. Disappointed in myself, I am willing to work on this particular problem every day. I do manage to go to my psychiatrist's appointment by myself during the week, so why can I not go to the grocery store, or for a walk in the park to relax? Besides my being anxious, I am not trustworthy due to my psychoses during the week, when I am alone in the house. On the weekends, my husband and I are together, so that he can watch me.

Happy New Year; this year really flew by.

My New Year's Resolutions are:

Isolate less
Work on going outside
No getting overly angry
Pray every morning
Exercise on treadmill
Eat right

These New Year's resolutions are important to me, because they give me structure in my life, and I know that I could never attempt these resolutions if I was not on Abilify, and feeling so well.

Dr. Sloan is on vacation for two weeks, which makes me feel apathetic and lost, yet everyone says that I sound great. I feel as though I am on an even keel, however, just below the living. Last night, all that I heard were screams, people talking, just mayhem due to my schizophrenia, and I could not go to sleep. I had to take an Ambien. I usually isolate myself, however, I did go for a walk outside both yesterday and today. Hopefully, I can continue this pattern and go for a walk outside tomorrow.

Tomorrow, I go to see my neurologist and I think that I need double the dose of Topomax, because my migraines have been occurring too frequently. The Topomax is supposed to stop the migraine before it starts, and I find that this dosage is not doing it's job anymore. I do not feel as though I am here or present in this world; my spirit is up in the clouds for the past day or so, and this is very annoying. I also feel as though I am not sure of myself. For example: I walked out in front of traffic twice today and thank God my husband held me back each time. I obviously cannot judge certain circumstances properly, and I realize that. I actually feel as though I am a scatter brain and I unfortunately cannot trust my own instincts.

Remember, that I have been diagnosed by my psychiatrist with having schizophrenia for almost all of my life, even though I am thirty-five years old now.

Keeping this a secret from everyone else was utterly difficult, but I managed to do this until I had my psychotic breakdown in 1999. Then the secret was out, and I felt as though a burden had been lifted off of my shoulders. Most of the people I told that I had schizophrenia were not sympathetic, and seemed to be apathetic to the news. I would have thought that the people I told, would have had more compassion, now that I had an explanation for my strange and uncharacteristic actions, however this did not come true. I would only enlighten my immediate family to my plight, if I had to do things over again, because they love me unconditionally. Even best friends can judge you and slowly remove themselves from your life. How sad, but how true.

All situations will work themselves out through prayer. Prayer is a powerful medium that we can use to communicate with the savior of the world. Just think of that for a moment, what kind of power we have at our finger tips. The more we give up our power to God, the more power we receive in turn from Him. When we tap into His greatness, we can actually tap into His world. See if you can devise your own prayer everyday because that would be powerful. God wants to hear more from his flock, and we are his flock. We are called his flock because in biblical times, sheep were wandering animals, as they are today, and did not stay in pack formation. However, when Jesus, with His staff, commanded that all of the sheep be brought together and follow Him, they responded in kind and became his flock. This is exactly the way we are; we are wanderers of the earth until Jesus calls us into his flock.

My brother called me last night and I am feeling great today because of that call.

Usually, I have tension in my voice, but last night I felt so natural and wonderful speaking to him. Really, I think that the longer I am on the Abilify, the better I seem to find myself. This is an unbelievable feeling of just relaxing and communicating with my younger brother (only younger by one and a half years). I would think that he heard a difference in me on the phone also, since it was as if two old friends were reminiscing.

My Godchild is making her first communion this weekend, so that my husband and I will be traveling to Rhode Island to experience the holy festivities. Oh well, I know that I will be nervous and anxious for this outing, because all of our friends and family will be gathered at my brother's home for a party. I really must meditate, just before I leave, and tell myself that I can just sit back and enjoy the day. I know that I have some extra Xanax, however I would like to handle this situation without taking any extra medication.

Let me just reiterate one point; when we have found the correct antipsychotic for ourselves, things will seem as if they are in focus. It feels as if we have just put on a pair of glasses with corrected lenses. Summing up this chapter, I might say that what I went through after I got home from the psychiatric ward was powerful. However, going through all of the struggles in dealing with the changing of antipsychotics for about two years, sticks in my mind as being extra demanding. Try to have a working knowledge of which medications you are on. You can look up the medications on a computer, and pay special attention to the side effects. Please do not forget to have your blood taken every three months to make sure that your kidney and liver function tests are in the normal range; also have your white blood cell count taken, because some of the psychiatric medications that we take, decrease the WBC count. Now it is fifteen years later since my first psychotic break and here is my medication list which I have been on for years.

AM	Effexor	225 mg.
	Xanax	3 mg. XR
	Cogentin	2 mg.
	Abilify	15 mg.
	Iron	325 mg.
	Omeprazole	40 mg

PM	Topomax	75 mg
	Cogentin	2 mg
	Abilify	15 mg.
	Latuda	20 mg
	Tricor	145 mg.
	Iron	325 mg.
	Vit. D	1,000 iu
	Omeprazole	40 mg.

These medications work like a well-oiled machine in my body, and I thank the Lord for my psychiatrist, who never gave up until we found the right combination of medications for me.

CHAPTER 5
PSYCHOSES

Psychosis is a state of being, consisting of our mind and soul existing in a world of non-reality. I used to find myself in the psychotic state quite often, the result of which I would desperately want to commit suicide, in both the state of existing in reality, and in non-reality. I still have psychoses, however, it does not lead to a feeling of wanting to commit suicide much anymore, because I have so much joy my life now, that I would never think of ending it. I find that having such joy, is the result of taking my medications diligently. What actually happens during the psychosis that I suffer from, even on all of the antipsychotics and support-ive medications I am on, is that I become an empty shell of a person, since my mind and soul seem to travel somewhere up into the stratosphere. I look for my mind and soul, but I cannot find them. I am not in my body as much as I should be. These episodes usually last between fifteen minutes, and can take up to a full day in order to finish. Here are some specific psychoses that I have suffered from.

When I was about sixteen years of age, my parents and I drove up to Canada to visit Quebec, Montreal, and Toronto. I could not believe how utterly cosmopolitan Toronto was, this was so exciting to me. Well, we found our hotel after driving around for sometime, and were very pleased with our accommodations. I, as well as my parents, had no idea what was to happen within the next ten minutes or so. This was to be my first psychotic breakdown, and it was miserable. This was clearly not my first psychosis I had been through however. We were all sitting in the hotel room deciding what to do first, when I felt an urge to get up, go to the bathroom, and lock myself inside.

Looking in the mirror, all that I could see were exaggerated features on my face and how ugly I was. I was sure that everyone would notice the features on my face. So while I was crying a lake of tears, I screamed to my parents that I was not coming out of the bathroom and to leave me alone. Hitting the wall of the bathroom while screaming profanity, I planned never to come out. My eyes started seeing my body in a tunnel like cloud, which I could not get out of. How utterly aggravating, and as a result, I started pounding my head on the wall for a few minutes. I was so frustrated. No matter how persuasively my parents spoke to me, I did not end up coming out of the bathroom for three hours. I never did tell my parents why I locked myself in the bathroom while steadily crying. They did not know that my features were all distorted and I did not want them to see me like that.

After I cleaned myself up and put myself together, we all eventually made it to the Toronto Zoo and unfortunately, all I could see was a black oily-type film covering everything I looked at. This scared me, because this is the first time I experienced this black oily-type substance dripping from everywhere; I felt as if I were in hell. I also felt like screaming derogatory remarks, so that we could leave because I just did not want to stay in such an ugly place. I did end up yelling a couple of bad words, however this was docile in comparison to what was really in my mind to do. I tried to keep myself together as much as I could. All I knew is that I was miserable, but I kept the visual psychosis of the zoo to myself because I did not think anyone would believe me anyway. I overheard my mother stating to my father that I had some definite problems, which should be looked at by a "head doctor". My father answered my mother, that he thought that this was just normal teenage behavior. Once again, my father missed an opportunity to take me to a psychiatrist for some sort of diagnosis, for what was truly ailing me. This is considered my first true psychotic breakdown, encompassing the scene in the bathroom, and the visual psychosis at the zoo. This finally came to a head, and then ended safely as soon as we left the zoo.

Other psychotic episodes occurred just outside of my apartment, as I began yelling at the people in the cars as they went by me. I would just go to the edge of the grass at my apartment complex, where there was a traffic light, and screamed derogatory insults at the drivers. Luckily, no one ever stopped to give me trouble. When I look back on those memories, I am surprised that I did not acquire any bodily harm from those drivers, because I was not yelling very nice things to the people who were in the cars stopped at the traffic light. Maybe, the people in the cars felt that I was sick, and thought it best not to engage me in a war of words.

Another one of my psychoses occurred when my husband and I went to a park we had never been to before, in order to walk some paths which were cleared in the forest. All of a sudden, I started seeing everything black and dripping with an oily substance.

Exactly like what I had seen at the Toronto Zoo. Not wanting to complain, I went along with my husband on the paths and commented on how beautiful the forest was. I needed to use the rest-room, and the park did not have any; so luckily we left, and my psychosis stopped within the following five minutes.

I had a psychotic break in a upscale restaurant, which I was invited to by my mother, and three aunts. We landed at the restaurant and everything was great, however, I knew that there was something not quite right within me at this moment. The waitress came over, and took our orders as we were all having a nice conversation. All of a sudden, I push my utensils onto the floor. This restaurant, of course, had to be full of people. I pick up my utensils and blame this on gravity. Once again, I push the utensils down to the floor and I proceed to pick them up again. My mother suggested that I leave the restaurant and go for a walk with her, and so I agreed. My aunt told me to go with her instead, so I got up and my aunt took my arm, as I started to kick various objects in the restaurant, all the way from the table to the door. She took me outside and the psychosis continued to play out. My aunt pulled me down the stairs to get me away from the restaurant, however, I proceeded to fall of my own volition and sat on the parking lot ground itself, just moving around on the wet pavement. Being upset, I wanted my mother there with me, so she came outside and so did my other two aunts, and we all left the restaurant together. How utterly embarrassing. Psychosis, like the one that happened in the restaurant, does not occur as much anymore, because of the wonderful medication that I take.

Another psychosis, that I experienced during some Sundays at mass, is that whenever I heard people speaking softly in the back of me, I was positive that they were speaking about me. So I turned around, gave them a dirty look, and continued praying along with the mass. When I heard people speaking out of turn at mass, it made me want to speak along with that person. Of course, my husband stops me, so that I do not make a complete fool out of myself. My husband is so tuned into my schizophrenia, and so I am very lucky to have him.

This is going to sound unrealistic, however, I am having trouble just hearing and listening to the correct words coming out of people's mouths. It is sometimes difficult for me to respond to a person's question, because I really cannot decipher the proper words and phrases that people say to me. Most of the time, it occurs because some people speak so very quickly and I just cannot catch on. Also, I cannot respond as fast as I should, due to having problems thinking of answers as quickly as I should. My cognition has definitely plummeted, and as a result, I miss just having a nice, easy conversation with another person. People actually must help me, in order to fill the proper words that fit into my sentences, so that I make sense. At times, I cannot even follow along to what others say, because I am actually struggling to think about each individual word, instead of the meaning of the entire sentence. This causes me to feel inferior to others and sad about myself. This also occurs when I am watching television; I do not seem to hear the correct words that are said. I am positive that not being able to decipher the correct words, has to do with either my schizophrenia proper, or the medications I take for my schizophrenia. I have never had this problem before, but now I do, and it is very noticeable.

I used to be very good in athletics, however now I cannot even keep my balance when I go to hit a tennis ball back to my opponent. Also, I used to be good on the trampoline, but now I simply do not have the coordination to jump on it. Another psychotic event happened in my psychiatrist's office. I am usually a meek, passive person; non-aggressive, and calm, except for when I am in the middle of a psychosis.

However, one day when I had an appointment with Dr. Sloan, I stood up, in the middle of our session, and confronted him. I told him that I was going to knock down the wall between his office and another doctor's office. Dr. Sloan asked me if I had taken my medications this morning, and I knew that I had not. Just wanting to be myself, without all of those pills, I decided to see what would happen if I did not take them for a few days.

Dr. Sloan stated that I was only myself, if and when I actually took my medications. He ran to get my antipsychotic medication for me and I started feeling better within a half hour. Dr. Sloan was wonderful since he did not stand up to confront me when I stood up to confront him. This was very important to me, since he kept me calm throughout this psychotic episode.

After I had been seeing my psychiatrist for about eight years, I was on my way to my next appointment to see Dr. Sloan. I remember being tired that specific day from all of the medications I was taking and not having slept well the night before. My mother happened to call me before I left for my appointment, and said that I could barely form any words, and that I should not drive to my psychiatrist's appointment that very morning. I told her that I must go to the appointment, because I had never missed one before.

Unfortunately, I had a psychosis in the car, and ran into a tree while I was traveling forty miles per hour. Well, my head was jilted forward and broke the front windshield of my car, and I suffered with other broken bones in my body also. I remember trying to get out of the car, but as soon as I stood up, I passed out. There was an ambulance, as well as about thirty people, on the scene. The ambulance attendants cut me out of my clothes, and that is all I remember until we got to the hospital. I later learned that my car was totaled, and as a result, I had to have a six hour surgery on my right wrist and I also had three broken ribs. Thank God I was in a very large car that protected me from the accident, otherwise I would have lost my life. I went to physical therapy for my hip and wrist, and continued to get better which took approximately ten weeks.

I will always carry the scar from this accident, on the inner portion of my right wrist. Interrogated by the police department as soon as I arrived home from the hospital, I was asked about the names of my medications, what they do for me in my body, and did I think taking these medications contributed to the accident. I told them no to that last question, and they told me that I probably should not drive again unless I had a co-pilot with me. If I had a co-pilot, I would feel much safer because the passenger could always grab the steering wheel in order to help me, if I went into a psychosis again. Since the accident, I really have not driven because it scares me.

Sometimes my eyes see something, processes it as something other than what it is, and as a result, I do not see what is truly there. For instance, if I happen to see a snake, I will look away and then look back at the snake, and it could turn out to be only a jump rope or something else long and malleable. This illness plays cruel tricks on the schizophrenic person. People and friends used to question me all of the time, by asking me if I was feeling alright. Even as I grew up, I heard these questions quite a bit. How are you feeling today? Or, is everything okay today? Since I was close to a few of my college professors, they would also ask me those basic questions. This made me think, that there was something wrong with me. I even had friends ask me those same questions and this used to get me frustrated. Until I found out that I had schizophrenia, I could not make sense out of those questions. However, the diagnosis set me free, because it gave me a reason why people had asked me those questions so frequently, and I finally knew that I was not quite the same as everyone else.

I remember going to my cousin's house one time. She suffered with schizophrenia, and she had asked my brother and I if we wanted a drink. We were only eleven and nine years old, while my cousin was approximately thirty. We said yes, a drink sounds great and followed her into the kitchen. While my cousin was pouring us some lemonade, she told us that when she dies, she is coming back as a cat. Well, my brother and I ran out of that kitchen so fast that we forgot our lemonade. I whispered in my mom's ear what had happened, and she told us to sit there quietly. I remember being very nervous, and wanting to go home immediately.

My husband, his sister, and myself went to Disney World for a nice vacation and one night we happened to close the park, and enter our assigned bus to get back to our hotel. Unfortunately, there was a four year old child sitting across from me, when I noticed that she was actually the devil. She was having a terrible temper tantrum as I suddenly heard the voice of the devil spewing from her mouth. The child-devil began speaking to me, so I closed my eyes but not before stating out loud that, "I know who you really are little girl." I remember my husband was trying to appease me, however to no avail. Finally, our stop was here and I practically ran out of the bus. Soon after, the psychosis left me.

Dr. Sloan asked me if I wanted to be part of a study group, in order for the psychiatrists to analyze a brand new antipsychotic, which was supposed to come out in the market place. This was a big decision, because once you get off of your antipsychotic and then back on it again later, you are susceptible to that antipsychotic not working as well as when you started it originally. Weaned off of my Abilify, I was placed in the double-blind study to see if the brand new antipsychotic would help me. I have to admit, the number of my psychoses, especially auditory, went down, however the new medication did not make me feel good inside, so Dr. Sloan, after two weeks, placed me back on my Abilify. Thank God that my Abilify worked as well on me after the study, as it did before the study. Allow me to state this truth again. We must never stop taking our antipsychotic(s), because when we eventually return to it, it might not work as well for us, as it did prior to getting off of it.

Seems as if the longer I am on my psychiatric medications, the less hallucinations I see, hear and smell. My psychiatrist does tweak my medications every once in a while, such as adding a low dose of Latuda to my list of medications, because I was having too many night terrors and still hallucinating. Latuda happened to be the perfect addition, because it has helped me control my emotions and decreased the number of my night terrors for now.

A good place to share my psychoses and other feelings I have running through my mind, is to divulge my story at a schizophrenics anonymous meeting. Dr. Sloan thought that I was well enough to attend a schizophrenics anonymous meeting, after being diagnosed approximately six months with my illness. So my husband, mother and I, all went to my first meeting. I asked if my family could please sit in on the meeting and the moderator agreed to let them stay for two or three weeks, since I was so shy. Being very nervous, I knew that this was an avenue to meet others, who had the same illness that I did, so I was willing to give the meeting a chance. I told the moderator of the group that I was not so sure that I had schizophrenia. He replied, that if I did not have schizophrenia, then basically we all, in the group, did not have the illness either. Not to hurt my feelings, however, I guess that it was quite apparent that I suffered from this illness.

Meeting people who had different forms of schizophrenia was very interesting.

There were approximately seven people in our group. Every week we would go to a church and have our meeting there; I rarely missed any meetings. Well, as time went on, we would hug each other after every meeting, and in no time at all, we became a closely knit family. There is nothing that I would not do for my schizophrenics anonymous friends, they have given me so much in return by sharing their stories. The sharing portion of our meeting is wonderful, because that is when one person at a time, tells us how his day or his week went, or really just what is on his mind at the time he is speaking. Another portion of the meeting I enjoy is that we are allowed to ask a limited amount of questions to each other and give each other advice. During this week's meeting, we exchanged phone numbers and made concrete plans to have a picnic at one of the member's homes. The picnic was very satisfying, because we played games together and learned things about each other, that we had no knowledge of before.

Schizophrenic people will always have their illness, because there is no cure for this illness as of yet. Schizophrenia is a very complex disease. It attacks all of our senses and brings the level of our cognition down. Personally, I have trouble with my short-term memory. This can be due to schizophrenia itself, the medication we take or a combination of both. Just two days ago, I had a psychotic event, which only lasted for approximately twenty minutes, however, for that terror-filled twenty minutes, I looked in a mirror and could only see half of my head with my brain hanging out of the other half. I became very irritable and unpleasant to be around. I thrashed my body around in bed with no control. Things of this nature might happen to you, even on your medications, especially when you are changing from one antipsychotic to another. This type of behavior is difficult to accept because we schizophrenics lash out at times, when we do not mean to. I used to be at the mercy of these psychotic events two to four times per week, however, now I get them two to four times per month. I am truly blessed. However I still hallucinate quite a bit.

There are different books out there which contain all types of research about antipsychotic medications, the different types of schizophrenia, and a multitude of other things. I highly suggest that each schizophrenic person should have these books, because the more we know, the better off we will be. Also, there is a popular web site for schizophrenics: www.mentalhealth.com, where we can communicate with others about our illness, or just sit back and read what others are saying about their experiences.

This is how I started, even before going to any schizophrenics anonymous meetings. I noticed that I basically had most everything in common with the folks on the web. The web site validated that I truly did have schizophrenia, which gave me a sense of peace and understanding about myself, however I still am not sure that I have this illness.

My husband was there, at my first meeting, when I actually had to say that my name is Nicole and I have paranoid schizophrenia. My husband also enjoys other meetings on the subject of schizophrenia. He reads various studies done on the illness and various information from the internet. He is very well versed on the subject of the illness, the pharmacological studies that are done on schizophrenics, and knows first hand the mind set and actions of a schizophrenic person, with whom he shares his life with.

Chapter eight includes four vignettes of various psychoses which are told by my friends who go to schizophrenics anonymous. You will see that psychoses take on certain characteristics for each of my friends, just as mine did in this chapter. My psychoses are brought about when my mind and soul escape from my body. Then, a psychotic event has a distinct possibility of occurring following the original psychosis, which happens when my mind and soul leave my body and cannot be found.

CHAPTER 6
MY JOURNAL (2003-2005)

I have been on Abilify for a while now, and I know deep within my heart that this is the antipsychotic for me. It makes me feel as if I am a person and the side effects are minimal. However, I still have visual and auditory hallucinations on the Abilify, but not as much as I used to. For example, I look upwards and I see the devil approximately twice per month. Sometimes he speaks to me, and at other times he is silent. The devil that I encounter has many different looks to him, at different times, and all of them are extremely scary. This I would say, is my primary visual hallucination. Obviously, I do have other hallucinations and horrific thoughts almost daily, but nothing frightens me more than the devil appearing before me.

* I went to my primary care physician today, and he said that I have low iron. I tried to take the iron pills he had given to me, however they bothered my stomach, even when I took the pills with food. As a result, I have been substituting red

meat and spinach for the iron pills. I remember when my cholesterol level was 298, just a few months ago because of the Clozaril I was taking. As a result, my primary care doctor placed me on Lipitor, which helped to bring down my cholesterol level. With no Clozaril in my system, and with the help of Lipitor, my cholesterol score is now 144.

* Still having terrible night terrors, I actually have a one way conversation with the people or monsters who are in my night terrors as I roll out of bed in the morning. I speak to them strongly, and ask them why they continue to torture me at night. My psychiatrist states that I should not dignify any of those people or monsters with any kind of response. He told me to completely forget about those people and monsters from my night terrors, because I am only wasting my time on something that is not real.

* I am having an awful day today, because I inadvertently allowed some bad spirits into my home by mistake. I opened the front door, just in order to breathe some fresh air, and the spirits took advantage of this situation and flew into my home. The weather is very dreary outside, and I am not present in my body. Again, unfortunately, I do not know exactly where my soul goes when it leaves my body every so often. My husband came home from work, and I was biting myself on the hand. He stopped me from doing so by raising his voice, as he came through the door. I bite myself to release some of the anxiety and chaos in my head.

* I thoroughly believe that there are spirits in my home and there is also rotting flesh in my walls. I want to desperately

call the police about this matter, however everyone I told about the rotting flesh in my walls, is against me calling them. I guess that I must be wrong about this, but sometimes I have olfactory hallucinations and cannot stop myself from smelling death in the walls. This putrid smell covers me from head to toe, and this is why I truly believe that there are spirits and dead people rotting away in my walls. " Is it not so tiresome to believe so genuinely in your hallucinations, such as smelling rotting flesh in my walls, yet no one else can smell it, or wants to believe that you can either?"

* When I went to see my neurologist yesterday, he told me that I looked great, and that I was speaking with less hesitancy. This made me feel as if I was on top of the world; what a heartfelt compliment. When those words came straight from my neurologist, I really sat up and took notice because he is a professional and has trained many hours in order to observe various changes in his patients. I was so very content the rest of the day because that compliment gave me so much confidence in myself.

* Bringing my older cat to the veterinarian is always a challenge, because she hates to go outside and as a result, growls all the way to the appointment. Unfortunately, my husband does all of the driving for us now, and I do not drive anymore because of my hallucinations. Sometimes, I happen to see people or objects, which are not actually present on the road. Therefore, driving at this time in my life, is not conducive to anyone, including myself and others. Returning to the information about my cat; we found out that she had an eye infection, she was overweight and

had arthritis. I cleared up her eye infection in no time, with the medication that the vet provided to me. I also placed her on a diet food, and she is doing much better now.

* I have this special prayer that I used to pray every night, and lately I have not been doing so because I believe this is just due to my laziness. When things are going well in our lives, it seems as though we do not call upon God to help us, because we feel as though we are in control and as a result we do not need Him at this specific time. However, He wants our attention, no matter what is going on in our lives. Unfortunately, we have no time for Him when everything seems to be going wonderfully. I would rather be a steady ship on a bumpy ocean; praying everyday, and offering up my day to God whether or not my personal circumstances are either good or bad. Laziness is not a suitable reason to pray less than I should. He has done so many noble things for me, as I am sure that He has done for you.

This medication, Abilify, is working better than any other antipsychotic that I have ever tried.

I needed at least two to three months for this medication to have made me feel better though.

Do not lose faith, because some medications take longer than one to two weeks, in order to become part of the fabric of our minds.

* St. Dymphna is the patron saint of mental illnesses and this is her prayer:

O merciful God, You have willed
That St. Dymphna should be

Invoked as the patroness
Of nervous and mental disease.
Grant that, through the prayer
Of this youthful martyr of purity,
Those who suffer from nervous
And mental illness may be helped
And consoled. I recommend
To You in particular
(Here mention those you wish to pray for).
Through Christ our Lord.
    Amen.

* My husband and I went to the beach with some fish and chips that we ordered.

We were feeding a few birds outside of the car window, until more birds came and attacked the car, just because they also were looking for food. It was as if I was in that movie the "Birds". We were able to have a good time because I took a Xanax 1mg. before we left, so that I would not be anxious. Medications are so important in my life now. I have finally accepted that taking all of these medications is slowly molding me into a more sane person. Remember that everyone of us is different, and responds to various medications in numerous ways. This is the reason that we are all on distinct dosages of assorted medications in order to aid our illness.

* God, I am so wonderfully glad that I am alive today. Although, there were some scary moments about two weeks ago, when I was alone thinking about suicide. I tried to call a friend in order to help me discuss my suicidal thoughts,

however, I got a busy signal, so I just sat on the couch until my husband got home, and I practiced positive self-talk and meditation. When my husband finally did get home, he suggested that we place the phone number of our local suicide hot line on the wall near the phone. You can find this number at the beginning of your telephone book, either under suicide or mental health. Mine was listed under suicide.

* I am doing great; Abilify, as well as the other supportive medications are working quite well for me, except for the little angry spells which I endure here and there. So, what I am going to attempt to bring up to my psychiatrist, is that maybe we should add 5 mg. of Zyprexa to my Abilify, in order to control my outbursts a little bit more. I hope that Dr. Sloan concurs with this because nothing ventured, nothing gained. Adding or taking away medication is all based on trial and error science, and how each of those mini-trials actually work for my schizophrenia, and which do not.

* I am doing well, because the negative symptoms are leaving me, but the positive symptoms are unfortunately not being controlled quite as much. In a way, I think that the negative symptoms leaving my mind, makes me finally feel better inside, because I have been able to find my true self. That I am able to put up with the night terrors and psychoses, is a trade off for feeling just as though I am a person who is centered and in balance, which is primarily due to halting of the negative symptoms. Negative symptoms describe feelings such as apathy and blunting of emotions. Positive symptoms describe such things as delusions and hallucinations.

* Instead of going to bed right away, I decided to go for my standard walk around the neighborhood. I always pray to God that I do not run into some acquaintance, because I enjoy being alone. I am better, however, I also have been slightly depressed, because I possess a greater awareness of my illness lately, which translates into strongly believing more and more that I am indeed a schizophrenic person. This means that I am actually growing in acceptance of my illness, however, I am suffering with each growing pain. Developing an opinion about oneself is predicated upon so many other notions and ideas other than if one is schizophrenic or not; this is a sound idea that I must always keep alive in my mind. I am a worthy person who contributes to a household both physically and mentally, day by day, and this makes me undeniably satisfied within myself.

* Sometimes I ask myself, " Who is anyone to tell me that in order to be "normal", I must take about eight different psychoactive pills per day" ? "Would I totally be psychotic off of my medications, or could I manage without my pills"? Well I did try to cut down on just one of my medications at night, and this morning I awoke feeling awful, totally apathetic.

I tried to catch up with taking this medication one-half pill every four hours, but as a result, I was not happy and balanced. This is why I would never stop taking my pills, even though they make me sleepy at times, this side effect is one which I can live with.

* Sleep is my number one problem in taking these psychoactive medications. I am up at four a.m. every morning, but need to take several small naps during the day. I know that

schizophrenic people tend to have a very hard time with their sleep patterns, including myself, but we should try and make the best of it. Literally, I am up every hour at night. I can never sleep throughout the night, probably because of my night terrors, and I know that this happens to many other schizophrenic people also.

* I went to get my haircut and I am fortunate since the hairdresser did a great job. Right now my hair is short and I am so relaxed. It is amazing how such a small change can make you experience happiness inside of yourself. Try and notice all of these small changes, because they will help you through the difficult times. It is not the big things in life which makes you most joyful, however, it is the smaller things that you have done on your own and have control of, which makes you content; have faith in yourself.

* Some construction workers are putting up vinyl siding on the complex I live in, and the machine, which powers the pneumatic gun, is very loud and right outside my window. This is a hard predicament for me, since I cannot escape the noise due to the fact that I isolate myself in my apartment and do not wish to go outside at all. Hopefully, the crew will be finished in a couple of weeks as they promised.

* Well, it is Saturday and I am pleased because I went out practically all day long, and I did not have to go back to the apartment in order to nap or meditate. This is very unusual for me. First, my husband and I went to Dunkin Donuts, next, we went to a golf range and I was really hitting the

ball straight. After golf, we went to the mall near our home, and then picked up some food for supper. God, thank you for this glorious day. Oh, and I was not bothered with any psychoses today, which helped immensely.

* Because I have gone to the grocery store every week, consistently, I know that I am getting better on my Abilify. I go every Saturday morning with my husband and I have not missed a Saturday morning in two months. This is hard for a schizophrenic person not to isolate oneself. When I first started going to the grocery store, I experienced a funnel cloud moving around me and everywhere I looked. I had tunnel vision, and people would dart in and out of the isles. The people would move in chunks of space very rapidly, instead of walking. I could actually hear the wind from the funnel cloud and this made me so very nervous. Now, at least that does not happen to me anymore unless I am very tired or very anxious.

* I am still exercising on my treadmill, but my hip started hurting lately. Exercise is so important for schizophrenic people, because of our slow metabolism due to our medications. As a result, we experience weight gain. I went to my primary care doctor for my hip pain and for my cholesterol check. As a result, the problem with my hip was tendonitis. The doctor gave me some Celebrex, which is an NSAID, and the pain went away.

* Tonight, I have been edgy all night, while moving my body parts around on the couch as I watched television. I cannot sit, I cannot stand, so I pace back and forth in my

apartment. Sometimes, I would walk round and around in a circle, which relaxed me tremendously. My husband was not home from work yet, and so I put myself in bed before I caused any damage to myself or my property. Being edgy is most probably a side effect of one or more of my medications, but I need every single one of those medications, in order to make me as present in the moment that I can be.

* Can you believe that I was just called in for jury duty? This is the second time within two years, that I have needed to obtain a doctor's note to excuse me from jury duty. I hardly think that the lawyers, who are trying the case, want someone with paranoid schizophrenia, who cannot decipher what is reality versus non-reality at certain times, to sit on the jury. Make sure that if you cannot go to jury duty, ask your primary care physician to place the nature of your disability on the form you receive, so that the county will not continue to bother you about coming in for jury duty.

* At 2:20 p.m. today, my Godmother died. This is somewhat eerie, because my father died at exactly 2:20 p.m. in 1993. Her death has really set me back emotionally; I do not feel the same without her on this earth. She is gone and I cannot believe it. At the end, she was on a very small amount of antipsychotic medication because she was crying out very loudly, as everyone could hear her throughout the nursing home.

Antipsychotic medication is not used strictly for schizophrenic people. However, it can be used for psychoses occurring in other diseases, such as: bipolar depression, AIDS and psychosis caused by prescription medication, amongst other illnesses.

* May is mental health month. I still have not been able to lose anymore weight.

I have been stymied at 174 lbs. for at least three months. I have been exercising, watching what I eat, and still no weight loss has occurred. Dr. Sloan stated to me that I should lose approximately one pound per month on Abilify. Basically, all of these medications are actually keeping me from losing weight, two different ways. In the first way, the medication slows down my metabolism and in the second way, the medication makes me hungrier than I used to be, and therefore I tend to eat more than I should.

* My husband and I met our family at church because our Godchild was making her first communion; what a marvelous celebration of Christ and the children. I do not understand why, but I was so nervous and anxious that I had to take an extra Xanax. The extra Xanax that I have in my purse is a 1 mg. ER, and it does a wonderful job of calming my agitation. However, I only take one pill when I am totally overwhelmed with anxiety and fear. Today, I believe that the anxiety comes from too many people being packed into a small church and just too many people being invited to the party afterwards. I actually had to go lay down upstairs twice; the first time, at which I took a nap, and the second time, I just needed to be alone. Everyone in my family is wonderfully supportive of my illness, so they do not question my intentions when I need to be alone.

* Since I had a little trouble with nervousness on the bus the last time I took it to my mother's house, my mother volunteered to take the bus up to my home, and then we would ride

back to her house together. What a great time we had: shopping, buying new clothes, buying a bathing suit, and breaking down barriers by staying out for a longer period of time than what I am used to. Usually, I would only make two stops in the stores before going home to rest, but this trip I was able to make four or five stops without becoming anxious.

* My cousin, who I speak to once a week from Washington State, sent me a beautiful fluffy bear through the mail. We have such a special spiritual bond. I am so lucky to have her praying for me, because she is so close to God, and I am able to learn so much from her. I call her my angel. She has prayed so much for me, just as my aunts have done also. One special aunt used to send me a note in a cute card every week, and I would look forward to that. This was to help cheer me up in the early stages, when I had just found out that I had schizophrenia, and I was not doing so well. I would like to take this opportunity to thank everyone who has kept me in their prayers. All of the prayers have helped me tremendously.

* I knew that this was probably not going to be the best of nights, since I saw hallucinations during most of the day. It seemed as if everything was running by me and through my head, as if we were at a movie, which was going much too quickly. I heard voices, which sounded like they were coming from a radio, as they were arguing back and forth. Hopefully, everything will calm down soon.

* God, you know what is in my heart, mind and soul. Please enable everyone who is suffering from some sort of mental or physical illness, to experience slightly more hope and to

be a bit better today. I understand that nothing is perfect except You, and we are imperfect as human beings, however, please have compassion on us, because we love You so much. We appreciate everything You have done for us, and please allow us to continue Your work, Lord.

* Do you know what is so difficult for me? I never know when I am going to experience a psychosis. Sure, sometimes I may feel a slight bit different right before I do suffer from the psychosis, however, this could happen to me when I am in my apartment, or it could even happen outside of these four walls, as it has done before. I wonder if this isolationism I deal with daily, has something to do with the fear of going outside, and experiencing some type of psychosis or panic attack. All I know is that I feel most safe and happy in my apartment.

* I am so thrilled that today is Friday, so my husband and I can spend the weekend together. He is my number one angel; so very comforting and special. I feel badly that I did not cook this evening, but when we went to sleep last night, my husband said that he also wanted to go on a diet. So, I figured that we would eat some Lean Cuisine with fruit for dessert. That should be enough food for us while starting on our diet. My brother and sister-in-law are also starting on a diet today. I, myself have been on a diet for four months already. I would like to lose at least fifteen more pounds, and my husband needs to lose about the same amount. It is difficult for us who suffer from this illness to diet because we are always hungry and hardly ever satiated. My husband is so good to me because he always says that I do not need

to diet anymore. Unfortunately, I know that I need to lose weight in order to be totally content.

* Part of my solution and path to success, is realizing the truth about where I am on this journey to "normalcy." I realize that I must keep taking my medications for my schizophrenia and my migraines both. I have established a regimen, at which I do not make many mistakes anymore, because I place the pills in my daily boxes. I have a day pillbox and a night pillbox, which is very convenient. The night pillbox is actually colored dark blue, so that I will remember that the pills in that box are taken at night. The day boxes are clear, so that I take these medications in the morning.

* My husband left me a beautiful card on my pillow, in the television room, stating his love for me, for no apparent reason. This made me feel so loved. Both my mother and aunt called me today, therefore, today feels as if it should have been a very special day. The moral of the story here is that, if you take the time to write a little card, or call someone on the phone, you can make someone else's day full of joy and happiness, just by reaching out; nothing extravagant needs to be sent.

* I have been apathetic for the last few days. I suppose that it has to do with knowing what will happen in the future about my having children. Sometimes I wish that my husband and I could have a baby, but both my psychiatrist and myself believe that I should not get pregnant, due to my schizophrenia. This would not be fair to the child. I always

wanted two children, but I do not seem well enough to take on this very precious role of motherhood. I am not stating that all schizophrenic women should not have children, but I am saying that I could not do it. Just for an example, there are so many things that go on in a day, that I do not recognize or realize and I know this because my husband tells me so.

For instance, yesterday I left the stove on and fell asleep. I know that you cannot do these things with children around, both falling asleep and of course, leaving the stove on for a long period of time.

* What is it that makes it so, that I awake happy and vigorous one day, but sullen and blue the very next day? Obviously, this is all a psychological problem. I must keep telling myself that the future will be bright, and give myself some hope that way, with positive thoughts and actions. I should try not to dwell on all of the bad thoughts that run through my mind, both day and night. I should go about my business, without multi-tasking in order to feel better. What I tell myself is that I know that I will be okay; I am only a slight bit depressed at the moment, so I will meditate and talk myself into a better mood.

* Pain in the lower extremities is debilitating. I will help as much as possible to relieve that pain from my patients. Being comfortable in our own bodies, is a most important subject matter, whether at school or at work in a hospital. I still remain utterly tenacious that one day, I will return to medicine in some capacity, I never want to shut any doors and that is why I keep my license current. Working hard to

pass my boards and licensing exam, I always have had the hope in my heart that I will work in my field again.

* I should never allow anger to dictate my thoughts, and as a result my actions also.

Sometimes I enter psychosis with anger and I curse out loud and bite myself. The most frustrating type of psychosis to me, is when my soul leaves my body and I am no longer present on this earth. This has got to be the most upsetting time in my day. I thank God for the schizophrenic medications being scientifically discovered, because they allow me to work toward organizing myself, my surroundings, and feeling more "normal" than ever.

* I feel as though I possess a thicker skin now. People cannot just read right through me, and situations that used to upset me, do not do so anymore. Others used to tell me constantly, not to allow certain situations to bother me. Well things do not aggravate me as much now. Feeling very, very sensitive, and keeping everything hidden inside of me before I had a psychiatrist, I now know that I needed to relive, rebalance, and give total control of my life over to God. Now, I see the goodness in people, even though I do have bad thoughts in my mind at times, I know that the thoughts are not real. Becoming better at deciphering reality from non reality is difficult for a schizophrenic person, however, I am on my way.

* As I stated, I am learning to deal with my emotions and stressors in life, better as time goes on. I believe that I have figured out, that it is better to release the stress I feel, instead of internalizing it. Fortunately, lately, I have been allowing my stress to come out, as the words just seem to roll off of my tongue, and I cannot seem to keep stressful emotions inside of myself anymore. I certainly do not want to offend anyone, but at other times, the stresses come out of my mouth easily as opposed to the occasions that they were kept internalized, so this is actually something new for me. The truth, however ugly it is, just seems to spill out of my mouth. It is all so brutally honest.

* God, thank you for my lovely husband, for he has been my main support system in everything I do and say. I have been living one day at a time and progressing one step at a time, which makes me serene. Multitasking is not healthy for people with our illness, because we only become more confused, very easily. Although I am still isolating myself at times, I am not making bad blood over it. The isolation does not bother me much anymore because I am just simply living my life and doing what feels right.

* Lately, my husband's high blood pressure medication has been changing his personality, ever so slightly. He is more combative than usual when we simply sit down, in order to have a conversation just about anything or anyone. Because he is also on cholesterol lowering medication, I wonder which of the two pills is causing him to be somewhat upset. I try to be very calm discussing our problems together, because two people with anger in their voices usually cannot work out much of anything. They just end up shouting at one another. Because I am struggling with my own anger problem inside myself, I will usually not say anything at the moment when the discussion escalates. When the problem

is basically solved, then I can express my true feelings to my husband. Things just work out for the better that way.

* If you have been given a new medication by any physician, to add to the list of medications that you have been taking already, ask the pharmacist if there will be any contraindications between the new medication and the older medication list that you have been taking. Also, try and manage to order all of your prescriptions from the same pharmacy, that way your pharmacist will know if there are any drug to drug interactions, considering all of your medications, and not just a few of them.

* God, I give up my day to You. I wish for what You desire from me. There are so many more sickly people than people with schizophrenia, and we do not have to look very far to see them. I pray for the people who are worse off than we are; some have had no food for days, others suffer from tremendous pain due to various maladies, and still yet, people that are mentally ill, but are in much worse condition than we, are due to the fact that they refuse to take their medications. I am also including the poor homeless people, who practically live in a state of non-reality (psychosis), because they either refuse medication treatment, or they do not have an opportunity to take their medications daily.

* It was Fathers' Day yesterday, and being that both my father and my father-in- law have passed, we made my husband the honorary father of our cats, who we treat like daughters anyway. It was fun because my husband played along with it. I

bought a new scale, because I did not like the way the older scale weighed me. Would you believe it, this new scale actually weighs me two pounds more than what the old scale did.

Obviously, I am still trying to lose weight, because of the weight I gained on my medications. I wish that I was not so quite obsessed with my weight, however, I allowed myself to go up to two hundred and five pounds and I remained this way for at least one year. Now, I am back down to about one hundred and seventy pounds; I am five feet and nine inches tall and I am looking to lose more weight.

* Crying for the first time today in a long time, I know what I am crying for, however, there is not much else I can do about it. I have paranoid schizophrenia, and this has affected every fiber of my being. For instance, writing and then typing this book would have been a disaster, if I would not have had a schedule of what I needed to accomplish for each and every day. Another reason why I am crying is that I must allow the other person that I am speaking with, to help me in order to find the correct words which will finish my sentence. Therefore, I am slower at speaking, I do not understand people who speak quickly, and at times, I cannot decipher their English at all, because it sounds like a foreign language. It seems that some of my faculties have left me, and that is why I was crying.

* God, I allow people to irritate me at times. These people are not worth my time worrying about them, but what can I do? What is it that they do not like about me socially? I do not know if I am being overly sensitive, or that maybe I am socially inept. People talk about me derogatorily, and that

makes me crazy. God, I can get along with respectful, good people, but I cannot get along with people who judge me, that do not even know me. I remember that God said something similar to this in the bible. If you love people who are nice to you and they love you back, where is the challenge and sacrifice in that. You should love people who are even your enemies, and pray for them, since they too have a soul given to them by God, just like you.

* My mother was not doing well for a short while, however, she is doing great now. She is on a regimen of about four different medications, which she gets from Canada, so that they do not cost her much money, because she lives on a fixed income. My husband has an excellent prescription plan from his work, because we have a one thousand dollar deductible at the start of each year, and then the insurance picks up one hundred percent of the medication cost for the remainder of the year. One thousand dollars is spent fairly quickly, especially when my Abilify costs over eight hundred dollars per month. Medications seem to be expensive in this country, versus in the poorer nations, who receive medications for a fraction of the cost.

* I never want to allow anger to dictate any of my actions. We are not on this earth for very long, however, when I think of suicide, I experience blackness and darkness, because I believe that I will be going to hell if I commit this action against God. However, if I pray and let things happen naturally, I know that heaven awaits me. I am an optimist and a realist. Being God's humble servant, I understand that there is a reward greater than I could ever imagine for

all people, who try their very best to be holy and to keep Jesus in their heart. Please God, never let me doubt that for a second.

* I have a dilemma; my husband took the first week of July off from work, so that we could go to Williamsburg, Virginia. Our family picnic on my father's side of the family is July fourth, in Massachusetts. My mother suggested that instead of going to Virginia, we could use her house as a hotel, go to the beautiful beaches in Rhode Island, and also go to Boston or New Hampshire for a few days. That way we could attend the family picnic. The truly wonderful experience here will not be where we go, but that I am finally well enough to embark on a vacation, and feel great about it. I remember the multitudes of times, when I could not even step one foot out of my apartment for weeks at a time.

* Well, I enjoy working out, because not only do I use the treadmill fifteen minutes per day, but I do ten very intense sit-ups also, for which I am starting to lose my little belly. I had always been thin at five feet, nine inches tall and weighing one hundred and twenty pounds, but now I find myself at one hundred and seventy pounds. My highest weight was two hundred and five pounds, and it took so much work to actually take that thirty pounds off. What started the ball rolling for my resolve to lose weight, one pound at a time, was that I happened to see a picture of myself at my highest weight and I barely recognized myself. Now, at least I look like myself, and feel like myself. This is why we should never quit trying to succeed, even when the task looks impossible.

When I went to my psychiatrists' appointment yesterday, he said that I could basically lose twenty more pounds. However, I wanted him to know that I was very comfortable with whom I was and what I weighed at the present time.

* Structure must be the basis of my life now, because it makes tasks easier, and less confusing in the end. Part of the structure governing our lives, entails that all schizophrenic people should carry a small calendar and pen, or an I-phone, so they may write down important information on their calendars. I have a big calendar, at home, one where you can write things on that you need to do. At home, I also write down all of my doctor's appointments, and in this way, the calendar becomes a type of journal. You can also write down what you would like to accomplish for that day. You will be happy with just those two calendars, and I know that this will make a substantial change in your life, because our memory centers in the brain are not as sharp as they once were.

* Currently, I am watching a documentary about panic attacks, and the people who have them. One lady on the documentary, has not been out of her house for four months; another lady has had to deal with five to six panic attacks per day. These women are living with a different illness than what we have, however, some of the symptoms seem to be somewhat like schizophrenia. Another lady stated that she leaves her body at certain times and she also recognizes the problems she has with isolation and forgetfulness. Although these symptoms have many likenesses to our illness, schizophrenia actually has many more symptoms,

which we must deal with on a daily basis, such as psychoses for a start.

* I went to a NAMI meeting last night, and the topic was "The Dynamics of Disclosure; it's Impact on Recovery and Rehabilitation". This was confusing to me at the beginning, however, I finally got the gist of it. We learned not to say that we have a mental illness, if we are applying for a job, or are on the job, or applying to schools. Also, we should basically only tell our immediate family about our schizophrenia, because they are the most compassionate people towards us and care for us unconditionally. We do not want to scare anyone away. To this day, very few of my family members even know that I suffer from schizophrenia, but what they do know is that I have a biochemical imbalance. There are good ways to tell certain people about our illness and bad, ineffective ways to tell them also. Please pick the former, we need to confide in people we trust implicitly.

* When I awoke this morning, I was so dizzy that I had to hold on to my husband in order to walk from one place to another. I looked up my medications in the Physicians' Desk Reference and found out that my Lipitor, Abilify, and Xanax all bring my blood pressure down, which can cause dizziness. Besides my possible low blood pressure, I have iron-deficiency anemia, and am currently not taking any iron for that. So, what I decided to do, was to call my physician and ask him if I could remove the Lipitor from my medications. The doctor agreed and later on that day, I finally felt normal again. I would not suggest that you take yourself off of any medications without consulting your physician. I will

have my cholesterol tested in about one month, without the Lipitor, in order to check to see if my cholesterol remains low, so that I can indeed stay off of the Lipitor and not feel dizzy anymore.

* I just came back from visiting my psychiatrist, and he stated that everything seemed as if life was treating me well. He was pleased to learn that I was starting a new chapter of schizophrenics anonymous, and that I had also participated in a NAMI meeting. My psychiatrist was also pleased with me, because I was writing this book to help families in crisis, who have schizophrenia and other mental illnesses.

* The Wimbledon tennis championship starts this week; as you can tell, I am a very enthusiastic fan of tennis. I always felt as if I had missed my calling in life, which was to become a professional tennis or golf player. Sometimes I lose my enthusiasm about tennis and that is where I can get into a deeper depression. My psychiatrist says that if I have something to get out of bed for, then I will be okay for the day. However, if I lose my passion for something that I used to love to do, and refuse to get out of bed for it, because I do not feel that there is any good things expected in the world for me that particular day, well, this can only mean that I am on my way down into a deep depression.

* Receiving an invitation to a party in the mail, used to make me quiver with anxiety, but no more. I received an invitation to a wedding shower, and I replied yes immediately. I also received a wedding invitation in the mail, and replied yes to that immediately also. I felt empowered. It is not that

I actually looked forward to attending these parties, however, I did not have to talk myself into going to the parties, or feeling guilty because I just could not make it. I was going to be seen at these parties, and that was okay with me. I just want to be myself, and that is good enough.

* I have been on Abilify for approximately seven months now. I went to the family picnic, on the fourth of July, which we have each year, and most of my relatives remarked on how alert and contented I looked. It felt so good to receive those compliments. I have great hope for the future, and for the present. The longer I am on these antipsychotic medications, the better I feel and act. There remains certain things that I am shaky about though, such as crossing the street, and forgetting simple words, but I call those my schizophrenic moments, and I try desperately not to let them bother me.

* My night terrors are still with me, even though I cut my Xanax down from two pills to one pill at night. I thought that just one Xanax at night might help, but it really has not. I never wake up refreshed, but that is okay. Unfortunately, there are so many other people suffering on this earth, it is incredible. Just for an example, I am currently watching the Amazing Race on television, and the show traveled to India, and maybe some of you saw what I saw; how poorly these people live. They live in cardboard homes, yet the parents send the children off to school in the morning, because they strongly believe in education. This really tugged at my heart strings, and I feel like a fool for mentioning my migraine headaches or the multitudes of symptoms that can

occur, due to schizophrenia. Let us go feed these poorest of the poor in India.

* We just came back from my mother's home, and I could actually keep up with all of the conversations I had with the other people there, even the fast conversations, it was amazing. I felt as though someone had turned a light bulb on in my head, and I could finally converse with whomever spoke to me. What a great feeling. I am getting better and better; I can feel it. My only complaint is that I tire easily, and must be alone for various parts of the day. When we take a nap during the day, our brains assimilate what has happened to us that part of the day. My brain needs that assimilation time.

* I bought myself a new bathing suit, even though I am not fond of getting wet anymore, since I started on my medications for schizophrenia. However, getting a sun tan at my brother's pool, was truly a joy and something that I have not been able to experience in a very long time. My sister-in-law prepared a wonderful feast for us to eat; and we did plenty of that because she is such a fantastic cook.

* Sometimes I enjoy scribbling down short quips of poems. Here is one I wrote very quickly:

Oh ocean so blue,
White sand that looks new,
Bathe my eyes in your beauty,
Make me feel gloriously,
Allow me to find my way,

Along the shore line today,
Hear buoys that chime,
I am oblivious of time.

* I am doing wonderfully. The little things, such as a virus infecting my body, and giving me a cold, used to bother me greatly. This does not bother me anymore, because I have been looking at the sunny side of things lately. I have such a positive attitude, and I am sure that my antidepressant has quite a bit to do with this feeling. I am ready to face any challenge that God presents to me.

* My husband stood by me when I was in the hospital for substance abuse, and at this juncture in our marriage, he stands by me with my paranoid schizophrenia. We truly realize what our marriage is made out of, when we only become stronger in the face of grievous reality. My husband is my best friend, lover, and strongest advocate for my recovery. My household is upbeat, because we truly believe that I will be getting better, and that is just a matter of time, including some hard work on my part. I look forward to every day with newly found courage, and I always offer my day up to God and pray that He uses me as He wishes and not as I wish.

* My husband and I went to see that movie, " Finding Nemo", and one of the plot lines was basically about setting a goal, having that persistence to follow that goal and gaining the results I want in the end. I see my life in that particular light because I set goals every day, and attempt to finish them. This makes me feel as though I should never quit, if I want something badly enough. Schizophrenia has taught me to

deal with life on life's terms, and to always put a positive spin on whatever I am doing. This works wonders for me.

* My husband and I went to church today, and the homily was so inspiring.

It was all about how to cherish giving, rather than receiving. Jesus gave all of Himself to the world, because God the father gave Jesus to all of us, to begin with. If we do not practice giving, we will never receive from the bounty of our Lord and God the father. I am not talking about specifically giving materialistic gifts, however, I am speaking of giving of our time and effort to someone who is in need of us. When we do someone a favor, it feels so satisfying, deep within our soul.

* It is such a gorgeous day out. The sun is shining, the temperature is perfect, and the birds are chirping. Today, my husband will drive me to a schizophrenics anonymous meeting. After the meeting, I will make a picnic lunch to eat on the beach, and then we will saunter along the shore line together. I am really looking forward to this. Yes, it is amazing that I actually look forward to these outings now, because I remember not so long ago, that I could not even leave my apartment. The new me is full of vigor inside.

This does not mean that I can always go out every time that there is an outing to attend, however, the percentage of my being present at these outings has definitely risen.

* The schizophrenics anonymous group which I belong to, is going to the Levitt Pavilion to watch the J. Giles band for free in August, which is happening very soon. The band

will be performing jazz, and the blues; this sounds most inviting. I enjoy heading out to various functions with my schizophrenic anonymous buddies. They make me feel comfortable and loved.

* There was a parade bisecting Bridgeport today and unfortunately, we were on the wrong side of the bisection to get where we wanted to go. My husband and I could not seem to make our way through traffic, in order to land on the opposite side of the road, which we needed to do, in order to attend my schizophrenics anonymous meeting, today. So we parked in a residential zone, and decided to walk across the parade route to the church. We promised the people at their residence, some tenants of that building who were outside, that my husband would be back in no longer than five minutes to move our car out of the residential parking space. My husband just wanted to be safe by walking me to my meeting. The lady sitting on the stoop, with a man, stated very sternly, that we should remove our car out of that parking space immediately, because those spaces were for residents only. The lady sitting on the stoop said that she was going to call the police, as soon as we left our car in one of the residential parking spaces, even if our car was only there for five minutes. I stated to her that I would never treat her and her car that poorly if she came to my property, especially if she promised me that she would be back in less than five minutes. She stated to me that she did not care what I would do. All my husband and I needed was five minutes to run to the church, where I had my schizophrenics anonymous meeting. We decided to take a chance, to literally make a dash for it, all the while long, knowing that the police were being called on us. How this ended up was that my husband made it back to our car and said a derogatory, " Thank -you" to the people who were giving us trouble, and he moved the car immediately, just as he had promised.

* Going for a walk near the ocean can be so cathartic and beautiful due to the sun shinning, the wind blowing, and the waves rolling in. A peaceful end to the day is God given. God, thank you for all that you have given to my husband and myself, while allowing us to keep a positive attitude and high hopes for the present and future. There are so many schizophrenic people, who are stigmatized, and not given a chance for a job, housing, or getting into good schools. I have high hopes for the new law, which just passed, and it states that a person with a mental illness, will be medically treated exactly as if he is a patient who has a physical illness. This law should really open people's eyes, and their hearts to our plight of living with a serious mental illness.

* I have just awakened, and I am still having my night terrors. They are absurdly awful and I wonder if they are caused by my medications, or caused by my schizophrenia which causes my night terrors. I have a feeling that the night terrors are caused by my medications, because before I started on these powerful medications, I never had night terrors this badly before. Unfortunately, bits and pieces from the night terrors, play as if they were on a CD in my mind; over and over again during the following day.

* The US Open tennis tournament is coming to New York soon. I cannot wait because I really enjoy watching the professionals go at each other on the court. Of course, I have

my favorite players, and I root for them loudly enough at home. Hopefully, my husband and I will get tickets to the matches this year. Having already been a couple of years to the matches, we had great fun, however, the good seats are quite expensive, so we bought tickets for the seats way up in the stadium, and we could barely see the players from all the way up there in the nose bleed section. So, even if we do not get tickets this year, the television crew does such a wonderful job with the commentary, showing close-ups, and giving facts about the players, that I think the best seat for us is right here at home, with some popcorn and drinks. It is so healthy for schizophrenic people to have something in which they really enjoy doing and actually doing it.

Otherwise, pessimism sets in, and depression is not so far away.

* It is imperative that we be interested in something in order to propel ourselves out of bed in the morning. I realize that I have just spoken about this, however, this is so important, that I wanted to reiterate it. Even if it is just as simple as a show on television, or a book that we are currently reading, we must always be interested in something. If we do not find that little something, we will start by mumbling to ourselves, " Why should I even get out of bed this morning, because there is nothing that interests me." We need to be happy about ourselves, as we should be. God does not make mistakes, but people do.

God created us in His own image, and He wants nothing more than to have us progress and do well. So, if you are having trouble in this department, meditate, pray about it, and start off slowly, taking one step at a time. You will find a substantial difference in your attitude, and you will actually love yourself more if you find something that you are interested in. I was one of those people who started out with no interests, and finally I started making a schedule for my day, and every time I completed something on the schedule, I checked it off and I felt a sense of pride as a result. These are the small steps that I am talking about.

* Finally feeling as though I am out of my schizophrenic haze for the first time in a while, I can speak to people without getting tongue-tied. I also enjoy reading again, I am interested in various things, such as cooking better food for my husband, and this regimen seems to be working for me so far. I hope that this feeling lasts for more than a few days. We can all leave the schizophrenic haze behind us with some work and prayer, because nothing comes without God. God is at the center of our universe, and is at the center of our lives.

* I am slightly nervous right now, because I need to call the main schizophrenics anonymous office, in about five minutes, to ask for permission in order to use the six steps from the schizophrenics anonymous handbook, which is used in our meetings, so that I can share these steps with you. Well, I called and unfortunately the director did not want the six steps in this book, because there were right to privacy issues. I see his point, I guess.

* Pieces of life must fit perfectly into a puzzle. Sometimes, all the pieces are in their places except for one piece missing, and in my case, this piece happens to be my poor

memory. Also, I am actually never empty inside anymore, since I have been taking Abilify.

Without Abilify, I would always live as if I had no life force inside of myself. Who was I? Now, it is a total difference. If the medication we are on is not working for us, let us not be afraid to ask each of our psychiatrists about switching or adding on a new medication to our regimen.

* My eighty-eight year old great aunt fell from a heart attack, and broke her hip.

She is a strong lady, because three days later she was in surgery in order to repair her hip.

I am so proud of her because she came out of this tragedy, better than when she went in for surgery. She did sustain some heart damage due to the heart attack, but she is feisty, and if anyone can get through this, she can. There is a lesson to be learned from this. We must all go through what God has given to us in our lives, in other words, what God has planned for us.

* Today, I am going outside and taking a walk. I have not been walking by myself in a while, because I must cross a major boulevard, and as you already know, this is very difficult for me. After I take my shower, I will go outside and walk. It is perfect walking weather; seventy degrees with not much sun showing, which I like because the sun will not affect my migraines. So, there is no excuse for me not to go outside.

Isolating myself can be stressful, because I know that I should be doing other things outside, but it is as if I am paralyzed, and I just cannot and will not go outside. However,

I know that I do not want isolationism in my life, therefore I will be going outside and I will force myself to do this.

* At the local Museum of Science, I went to see a movie about the Australian Great Barrier Reef with my husband. I was mesmerized. The movie displayed incredible lighting, vibrant colors of living organisms, and spectacular beauty across the entire reef. The venue was an IMAX theater and I felt as if I were diving into the ocean myself. I would absolutely want to go snorkeling along the Great Barrier Reef, if I had that chance. We all must keep our dreams alive, because they just might come true. Just the coral and what lives in the coral was stunningly beautiful. There was something that popped out quickly from a piece of coral, and although it resembled a fuchsia colored flower, it was actually a type of seaweed. This was spectacular, not to mention all the different types and sizes of fish swimming about. My favorite was the parrot fish.

* Sometimes, people seem to speak so quickly, that I feel as though I am about to experience an out of body moment. My mother can be one of those people. She does not mean to speak so quickly, but sometimes I just cannot keep up with her words and sentences. I try and hide my nervousness as best as I can, although I suppose that is not the best answer for this problem. Maybe I should try speaking to her again, about speaking so quickly, and hopefully this time she will understand.

* Well, we have cigarette commercials on the air again. The cigarette companies are so ingenious, that they place

their ads disguised as, "There is no safe cigarette"... so millions of viewers can hear about cigarettes on a regular basis again. I believe that the more you talk about cigarettes, the more people want to continue to smoke or try it for the very first time. That is a principle of advertising. Everyone knows by now the dangers of smoking, but that stops very few candidates from quitting. So yes, I do think that this advertisement is done in a very sneaky manner, but to our detriment. I know many schizophrenic people who smoke and I wish that they would quit. Now, we have many resources to aid people in order to quit smoking: nicotine gum, nicotine patches, medications in the pill form, among other solutions. Cigarettes are made up of many carcinogens which attack our bodies. I am not quite sure why people who suffer from schizophrenia have such a high smoking rate, however, I wish all of you luck in possibly quitting this nasty habit.

* Here is another small poem that I wrote:

> It's a beautiful day,
> Won't you come out to play?
> Angels abound,
> Where God is found,
> Everything is right,
> With all of God's light
> Let's come together and pray,
> Life will be better today.

If you feel good, you might want to start your own chapter of schizophrenics anonymous, if you are well enough. Post signs in the local hospital and in the local paper, because relatives of the schizophrenic patient, or the schizophrenic patient himself might be reading the paper that day, and be interested in your meeting. It is however better to start off in your own phone book for information. For instance, in the yellow pages under mental health, they list family services. This would be a good place to start.

* This book has come full circle. The manuscript started off about a scared, anxious young girl, and now a more organized, wonderfully happier adult woman has emerged. I am pleased about what I have accomplished so far. My hope is that all of our schizophrenic friends will read this book, even if they have to pass around one copy between them. I want to provide assistance to as many people as I can; this is my definite goal for this book.

* There are many signs of schizophrenia and the psychiatrist knows them best.

As a parent, do not be afraid to ask your child or teenager if they see or hear things, which turn out to be unreal or just do not make sense to them. Do they seem overloaded all of the time, or do they say that they do not look like other kids? Prod them, but in a gentle manner, and if you have a teenager constantly spewing out that he wants to kill himself, then please go straight to a psychiatrist. Do not wait!

* Beauty is all around us, even when it is raining, which gives our wonderful trees and grass much deserved water. I marvel at our gorgeous sky, and our puffy white clouds. Do

you know what makes our sky the color blue? It is the reflection of our deep blue ocean on the sky. Just imagine all of the life there is in our wondrous oceans; so deep, so strong, and yet controlled by the moon up above. Life might have come from the big bang, but certainly God had to have set all of those gases in motion; swirling furiously, spitting out galaxies, stars, black holes, super novas, etc. (How spectacular). Life is certainly bigger than all of us, but we are all responsible for ourselves and our brief life that we live here on earth. Hopefully, it is a good life, as we represent together, a large class of people who have the unbelievable burden of our illness, but tremendous resolve in order to aid ourselves. We need more research into our illness, because I believe that the future of curing schizophrenia is almost here. In my opinion, gene therapy will play a major role in finally conquering our illness, schizophrenia.

CHAPTER 7
EXPERIENCES (2013-2015)

Do you remember when I told you that I was in the psychiatric ward many years ago for being detoxified off of my painkillers, and I felt as though God and Jesus had abandoned me? I have experienced this most sorrowful type of death in my mind, only twice now. However, I am sadly undergoing this tragedy again for the third time.

Specifically, there is nothing but a black hole, where God's love should be shining brightly in my soul. So lately, I have been praying to God passionately, however, my mind and soul is devoid of my Creator. The devil is rampant, and I could not find my maker at all, for the better part of four days. I know that God's love is missing in my life, and I am not sure why this is so. Feeling as if I am in space, in total darkness and alone, I keep crying out for God, but to no avail.

Since God was missing in my life, one morning at 4:30 am, while I was visiting my mother in her retirement home, I got up out of bed, I left my mom's apartment, and went for a walk because I could not sleep. While heading downstairs, I felt some attraction pulling me towards the chapel, as I passed by. I sat down in the chapel, staring at the cross on the altar, and begged God that He give me the belief that I will be with Him now and forever.

Staying for a rather lengthy time in the chapel, God answered my question about Him filling the hole in my soul with His love. He stated that I will be with Him forever, because I am His creation and I belong to Him. He is my Father and He will never abandon me. I was thrilled because God was back in my life. I could hear and sense His omnipotence.

Still in the year 2015, I usually make a concrete list for what I need to accomplish every day. I feel so good when I finish a day's worth of chores. I was not quite finished my chores one day, and I decided to take a break and call my aunt; we keep in touch and she always has something interesting to say. After I dialed her, I heard the ringing of the phone in my ear, and then she answered the telephone. I sheepishly stated to her that I have paranoid schizophrenia. She answered in a confused voice, " All of us know that you have had schizophrenia for many years now, Nicole". At first, I cautiously received and processed what my aunt told me. I wanted to believe her, however, I did not understand how I could have been fighting the realization that I have had schizophrenia for such a long time.

Unfortunately, I do not have the self-introspection to understand that I have this illness.

I was telling myself that there was no way that I have this illness, from the very beginning when Dr. Sloan diagnosed me. Dr. Sloan told me, that I had been fighting this diagnosis, since he revealed it to me some fifteen years ago. I believe that many people could not even tell that I had not accepted schizophrenia as my illness, because I owned the illness as if I had it. However, down deep inside myself, I really never believed that I had schizophrenia, even though I possessed all of the criteria for the illness.

I am still having trouble taking showers, because I do not like getting wet. I write a big S (for shower) on my calendar every three days, and I make sure that I always smell clean. I do not even enjoy swimming anymore, whereas I used to swim as if I were a fish, a very long time ago. I was even asked to join a pre-Olympic team when I was just eleven years old. I used to love the water, however, schizophrenia has taken that love away from me. I am relegated to feeling strange and uncomfortable in water, which occurs when I take a shower every three days.

Halloween is coming up soon and I do not enjoy that holiday. There are gory masks and costumes. My worst fear of Halloween is that the monsters that walk around as if they are dead, will attack me in some manner. My husband tries to explain to me that Halloween is only used to make money for the economy, and also only lasts for one night. However, this does not help me much, because I go into a panic attack every Halloween. When it comes time for the kids to collect candy, we have our lights off, no television playing, and no noise or light coming from our house. This works rather well, since no one knocks at our front door on October 31st.

My family went on an Alaskan cruise a couple of years ago, and I was actually able to go and enjoy myself. We saw whales, bears, and moose all living successfully in their wild habitats; how glorious. Every year we also have a wonderful family reunion; a clamboil, which I missed going to a few years here and there, either due to psychosis or other bad feelings and thoughts that I had, which made me very nervous and sad. As a result, I was not able to leave my home. Well, I happened to go this summer to the annual clamboil, and several family members mentioned to me how genuine I seemed, and how I had no problem speaking to anyone there. One family member even stated how I seemed to actually like myself, and how my newly found confidence was refreshing. Before I went to the clamboil, I talked to myself and I came to the conclusion that I would just be myself, and that was good enough for me. Being myself was the most important ideology that I actually learned that day. As you have read, the years 2013-2015 has had some ups and had some downs, just akin to anyone else's life. Life happens as time rolls on, but I am more equipped emotionally to deal with life on its own terms now.

I expressed to Dr. Sloan this year, that I was truly forgetting words and ideas when I spoke, and I wanted desperately to know if this was occurring because of my schizophrenia or could I possibly have the beginnings of dementia? Dr. Sloan was kind enough to give me the information of a doctor, who dealt with this very question. I was so ready for a professional to ferret out this answer. My husband and I went to see the specific doctor that my psychiatrist had referred me to, and he asked me some questions for approximately one hour. After that was finished, he told us more of the specifics of the written test that I was to take the following Saturday. All of a sudden, I heard this doctor

tell my husband loud and clear, that he thought the problem stemmed from all of the different medications which I
was taking. This apparently drove down my cognition and
memory centers, and that was his diagnosis. So why should
I make a second appointment to this doctor's office in order to take his test when his mind was already made up? I
needed a doctor who had an open-mind about the test, of
which I had not even taken yet. Needless to say, I never went
back to that doctor. My psychiatrist believes one hundred
percent that my forgetfulness comes from my schizophrenia and he does not believe at all that I suffer with dementia. That diagnosis is good enough for me and I stand by
what my psychiatrist states.

This year, my husband and I have traveled and visited
relatives, more so than at any other time during our twenty-
three year marriage. I was always so sheltered (of my own doing), just wanting to be alone in my house, and could barely
ever go out anywhere. Schizophrenic people seem to look
for a place, in which they may remain comfortably without
others. Now, that I prayed and forced myself to be with other
people at parties or simple gatherings, people seem to appreciate me trying so very hard to be with the rest of the crowd.
My brain must process what has happened both to me and
to other people during the first part of the day, however. To
achieve this, I will go into a quiet bedroom in the home I am
visiting at the time, and close my eyes for a half an hour or
so. This helps me tremendously in order to assimilate what
has transpired earlier in the day. Then, I usually come back
to the gathering with a fresh attitude after I awaken.

Also, my medications do make me tired, and my relatives
and friends understand that I must go into a quiet bedroom

in order to sleep or meditate. I believe that I have adapted my behavior, as best as I can, when I am around other people. I am genuinely content to be with other people, which is such a new joy in my life now.

My Godfather past away and thoughtfully left me a small inheritance. The lawyer who was taking care of my Godfather's will, who happened to be a longtime friend of the family, absconded with not only my inheritance, but with my aunt's inheritance also. I was able to call the City Hall of the state in which the crooked lawyer lived, ask them what I needed to do to collect our money, and to please forward all of that paperwork, so that I could start filling it out. Well, I was able to actually fill out the paperwork on my own without any lawyer present, and I eventually sent the paperwork back to City Hall. I called City Hall again, and they told me what my next move was. Anyway, I reached the point to where the lawyer, who stole our inheritance, was going to have to face me, my aunt and the judge in a courtroom, if he did not pay up.

Warning him over the telephone that I did not want to see him in court, I spoke nicely to him and he stated back to me that he promised that the checks to my aunt and myself would go out into the mail soon. I was pleased, however, this never actually occurred. We did not receive any money from my uncle's estate. Unfortunately, since I lived in a different state than the crooked lawyer did, I had to stop all communication regarding him. The reason being was that I needed to be available to the court, at a moment's notice and that could not be done logistically, simply because we were two hundred miles apart. I could have never gotten this far by myself, filling out law paperwork and speaking to the crooked lawyer on the phone, if it were not for taking my medications dutifully. My cousins, my aunt's daughter and son, actually took over the case where I left off. With a new lawyer (on our side), my cousins and the new lawyer were able to force the crooked lawyer, to actually give both myself and my aunt our inheritance checks after all. The lesson here is that schizophrenic people can make a difference and figure things out by themselves. We can be very insightful and helpful to our own causes.

My mother, an adult education student through our local university, invited me to go on a glorious trip to France a couple of years ago, since the students and the professor of her French class were planning on going soon. All of us would fly to France simultaneously, and spend our beautiful European vacation together. This sounded like such a special time for both my mother and I to bond even closer than we already were. Of course I agreed to go with her, and I was thrilled to be asked to go to France, by my mother. The night before we were ready to leave, both of us packed feverishly to get ready for the big trip. The sun rose and morning came, the limo company was outside waiting for us, and so I brought all of the luggage and bags out to the car. I asked my mother if she was sure that she had all of her paperwork ready to go in her purse and she stated yes. I checked my passport etc. one more time as we climbed into the limo, and so now, we were off to Logan Airport. When we arrived at Logan, the driver took our luggage and bags out of the car, and said to us, "Have a great time". So, we proceeded to find the rest of the French class in the airport, and stood in line with them in order to be processed to fly into Europe. We were already the next people in line up to the counter, so I asked my mother if she could take out her passport, plane ticket, and all of the rest of the paperwork pertaining to our trip. All of a sudden, I hear from my mother's voice, "Oh no, I cannot find my passport". I said, "Wait a minute and let me check", and so I completely emptied her purse on the counter and sure enough, no passport. Well, we ended up checking every single piece of luggage and bags for this passport, but to no avail. It was not anywhere to be seen.

In a panic, we asked the lady at the counter, "What should we do"? She said that if we found the passport and could get back to Logan tomorrow at the same time, then she would honor our tickets for the same flight the following day. We thanked her profusely for her patience and kindness. So, I called my brother to tell him the story, and because he was working in Boston at the time, he came to rescue us at the airport, and we proceeded to go back home with him. When we entered my mother's house, we looked hours upon hours for that passport, until I was feeling just a bit warm in the room I was in, so I went to open the window, and I do not know why, but I happened to look down in the trash can, and there it was, my mother's missing passport. We figured out how the passport actually landed there, and proceeded to make arrangements in order to travel back to Logan Airport the next day. Once I did that, I was at peace. My mother had the beginnings of dementia at the time, so I knew that I had to be the leader of where we were to go and what we were to do. I also managed how to get us from the Airport in Ireland, to the Airport in France, and then to a small town in France, two hours away where everyone else was located.

I was very pleased that mom and myself were able to make our connections because I know for sure that I could have never handled this situation about five years ago. We had a wonderful trip and I am getting better and better each and every day. You too can handle problems of this sort, if you keep in mind a positive outlook, and take your medications faithfully.

I am from a cozy little town on the east coast, where nothing really dangerous usually occurs. In high school, I was a good student, so I easily made friends with a few of my teachers, while I was growing up. Also, this is where my father taught the French language; he was actually the department chairman of foreign languages. Two of these teachers in my father's department were married to one another. They had two beautiful children, a son and a daughter. The son was diagnosed early with paranoid schizophrenia. Well, as the son grew up, he would at times take himself off of his medications, but his parents always managed to talk him into re-taking his medications for his own good. Unfortunately, the son decided that he did not need his medications anymore, ever. When his parents had discovered that he had not been taking his medications for a while, it was too late. He brutally murdered his father and desperately tried to kill his mother, but he was unsuccessful at slaying her. However, since he has been back on his medications in prison, his mother has totally forgiven him because he was so very sick when this rampage occurred. I do understand the son's point about stopping his medications because of their side effects, however, what a sad story this is.

I am not so sure of my own movements and motions of my body anymore; I do not trust myself. Being clumsy and awkward has never been part of my modes operandi.

I have always been athletic and in shape. Finding myself tripping over my own sneakers had never happened before. Also, I have trouble just jumping on a basic trampoline in my brother's back yard and this certainly has never happened before either. When I played fast pitch softball, as a pitcher, I had one of the best arms in the league. Now, I can barely throw the softball to another person just a few yards away; very disappointing.

I used to pound on my neighbors walls and scream towards their apartments, just because I would hear various noises coming from the other apartments. All of these symptoms could not be controlled, however, I started on a new antipsychotic in 2015, called Latuda, and that has given me the strength to act much more "normally" (without so much psychosis). I am thrilled, because I used to bite myself and I no longer do that either. Thank You Lord.

Lately, I still have been having trouble with remembering memories, such as I cannot remember what I did yesterday or even what I ate today at certain times. I also have trouble speaking with others, due to the fact that I just cannot remember basic words to converse with. Although some days are better than others, when I am speaking, the other person must interject the correct word that I mean to say, and this becomes very clumsy; I struggle with this even today.

I give myself over to God each and every day, to do with my life what He pleases and not necessarily what I please; let go and let God. God, thank you for the opportunity to struggle, recover, and then be given the Holy Spirit in order to grow closer to You. I do not know what the Almighty has planned for me, but I do know that I would like very much to work part time in some capacity in the future.

Night terrors are horrific nightmares which one re-members all night long, and lives many times over during the following day. One night while I was asleep, there were hundreds of rats eating the flesh off of my body, and my skeleton was starting to become apparent. I could smell the rats, listen to their high-pitched squeak, and I could actu-ally feel them scurrying all over my body as they nibbled away at me. Another night terror that had occurred when I was laying down fast asleep, happened the very same night. I actually had these huge snakes coming out of my mouth. As I am pulling them out, in order to try and rid myself of them, I noticed that these huge snakes were muddy looking.

However, there is something which I do discover all the while I am pulling them out of my mouth. I actually real-ize that these snakes are no snakes at all, but they are my large intestine. Not knowing what to do, I tried diligently to shove all of my large intestine back into my mouth in or-der to swallow it. I started choking on my intestine at this point, which happened to awaken me. These two night ter-rors are just a mild example of what I endure throughout the night.

We should become very familiar with the medications that we are taking. Did you know that grapefruit juice is contraindicated with most antipsychotic medications? If we are having a new prescription filled or buying a medication over the counter, it would be worth our time to ask our pharmacist if any of our medications would be contraindicated with the new medication that we are having filled or buying over the counter. I had this exact situation happen to me; unfortunately, I had forgotten to ask the pharmacist about how my new medication would react with my medication profile. By the time I got home, I had received a call from the pharmacy warning me not to take the new medication. Needless to say, my doctor had to replace the new medication with another similar type of medication and everything was fine.

As I am writing to you this very minute, I am actually struggling with the feeling of committing suicide, for the last three days. The struggle is intense, however the intensity has been lessening each and every day. Not knowing where this feeling is coming from (because I am happy in my life today in 2015), it is still quite difficult, but not impossible, to talk myself out of wanting to end my life so abruptly. Slowly but surely, coming out of the darkness into the light on the fifth day, and knowing that I would go straight to hell if I did commit suicide, I was ready to embrace life rather than death.

God also makes us a promise that we will indeed join Him together forever, with our Lord in heaven. I am ready to meet my maker at anytime, however not at my own hands, but only when God is ready for me. Remember, ten percent of all schizophrenic people do commit suicide.

A few days ago, I do remember that I saw the devil flying through the air, and all of a sudden, speaking loudly into my ears. However, the devil does not always speak English, but he does speak in some guttural and gruesome noises to me, which I unfortunately understand. This had all happened a few days ago. However in a certain way, I am used to all of this chaos, so my suicidal tendencies are probably stemming via different circumstances than from my schizophrenia at this point. I wonder if seasonal affective disorder is bothering me, and my strong feelings of committing suicide is just part of this disorder?

Well, I was able to cross something off of my bucket list, when my whole family took a wonderful vacation to New Hampshire. Seven out of the nine of us actually planned to go on a zip-line. This was my first time, however other people in the group had already experienced this unbelievable feeling before. Never so scared in my life, I was the person who held up the group, because of my nervousness at every new zip-line coming down the mountain. Feeling as if I was totally in a trance as I embarked on my first zip-line, I needed reassurance from the rest of the pack. They were wonderful, telling me the easiest way to let go, and travel at thirty-five miles per hour over the tree canopy. I did it for the very first time! Can you believe it? I, who was so very scared just to come out of my home, not so long ago, am actually on a zip-line? Now all I needed to do, was to participate in longer and more advanced zip-lines, all the way down the mountain. Yikes! Another part of this experience that I was not told of before we went up the mountain, was that we all needed to repel down the faces of trees which were approximately sixty feet high. Again, this was so nerve-racking and to this day I do not know how I made it. After the apprehension of zip-lining was over, I was never so happy to be on terra firma. However difficult this experiment had to be, I was proud of myself, because I did not hide in a corner when the rest of the people on our trip asked me if I wanted to go zip-lining. I did it just like everyone else. Yes, just like everyone else.

My medications certainly had worked, and given me the mental strength to participate in an unbelievable experience. I could have never accomplished this activity, if I was not on my psychiatric medications and had not been to Dr. Sloan for his advice all of those many years. I was thrilled.

Lately, I have been listening to the, "Natural Relaxation" CD's, in order to let go of the ugly thoughts in my mind, clear my head, and fill it with soft, beautiful music. I would suggest to anyone of my schizophrenic friends to buy a meditation type of CD, and allow the CD to fill the chaos in your head with lovely, relaxing music. We as schizophrenic people have so much chaos interfering in our heads, that we could use this kind of CD, in order to replace some of the psychosis (whether seeing, hearing, or smelling), which we usually experience on a daily basis. This has helped me tremendously. Keeping our mind busy with soft music, allows us to concentrate on just the CD, instead of thinking of grotesque imagery. It also helps us to decrease the anxiety associated with psychosis.

My husband and I were invited on a cruise ship, along with the remainder of his family from Venezuela, in order that we may all be together. We have not seen some of these relatives for the past fifteen years. We have wanted to go to Venezuela desperately, in order to visit my husband's family, however, the American Embassy has issued a bulletin against Americans visiting Venezuela, due to the dictatorship, which currently runs that country. There would be a possibility that we may not be let out of the country, once our visit was over. So, this will be so exciting to see the rest of his family, in a safe environment. My husband's sister thought of the idea of being together on a cruise ship, and we will be flying into Aruba, in order to board this cruise ship. This wonderful trip will take place in this year 2016, however, we must make our decision quickly if we are going, because my sister-in-law needs to order the tickets very soon, in order to save nine spots for us all.

Usually, when a trip such as this comes along, an invitation for eight nights away from home, my husband and I would most probably say that we could not participate, due to bad thoughts, and psychoses on my part. However, since I have been doing so well, we do not have to discuss these matters at all. Even if I do suffer from psychosis, my husband is not worried, since I have more control over certain types of psychoses, such as screaming out loud in a public place. I know that this can be very embarrassing. I am so ready to go now, that I really want to start packing immediately, even though the trip is not for a few months yet.

Unfortunately, my mother continues to have dementia and is getting worse by the month. I still visit her for a whole week in her independent living facility, every two months. We are the best of friends, and we enjoy each other's company. I help her out as much as I can when I go see her, such as cleaning and changing her closet over to the next season's clothing, and helping her do some of her errands. We keep in touch on the phone by calling each other approximately four to five times per week. She does repeat the same words and phrases over and over again, and my psychiatrist does not think that her company is the best place for me, since I am schizophrenic. However, there is truly a strong bond between us and we love each other so much. I am a compassionate person by design, and I feel good when I can help my mother, by finding lost articles of hers and whatever else she needs me to do for her. Sometimes, I am the one who actually needs help with my vocabulary, so she fills in the correct word when I need her to complete my sentences.

Still not holding a job in the year 2015, I am still not well enough to handle the public on my own or leave my house every day for a certain amount of hours in order to work. This would be much too uncomfortable, and I find myself having too many psychoses just now. I am not quite ready for a job yet. However, I know that some of my sisters and brothers who have schizophrenia must work no matter what befalls them; either none of their families step up to aid them financially, they are not married, or they cannot collect social security disability for some reason. I am so grateful that God has blessed this union between my husband and I, and has given me a partner, who is not only my best friend, but also understands my illness so well. I told my husband many times, that if he were the person that was disabled in the marriage, I would have kept my job at the hospital with no regrets. I would have financially taken care of us, just as he does for us now. Maybe a successful way to begin working, would be by volunteering at a nursing home, so that I could go in when I feel good, and stay at home if I have a bad day.

Hopefully, there is a nursing home near my house, because as you know, I should not be driving due to the major accident that I had, hitting a tree head on, going about forty miles per hour. Possibly taking a taxi cab to the job, as long as the job was not too far away, could also be an option. I absolutely enjoy the company of the elderly and would love to wait on them hand and foot. Therefore, maybe this is in my near future. Listening to the elderly speak about their past is so interesting and informative. I realize that some of them have dementia, and repeat stories over and over again. However, allowing them to repeat their stories and seeing the joy in their eyes, would engage me to listen to them even more. The nursing home environment seems to be a good fit for me and I will truly look into this.

Now, if I could only sleep somewhat better at night. Every night I walk up the stairs in order to go to bed in my home, and hopefully to remain in bed throughout the night. However by 11:30 pm or 12:00 am, I find myself walking back down those same stairs, back into the family room, because this is where our television is located. Laying down on the couch and watching three to four hours of television over night, I still remain able to rise at 5:30 am with my husband, so that I can make the bed and his breakfast before he finishes his shower. I actually arise at 4:00am in order to eat breakfast, take my medications, wash up, and change my clothes. I believe that this is one of the reasons why I need to take several short naps during the day. Struggling to sleep at night, can be a symptom of mental illness, if other diagnoses are ruled out. Once again, schizophrenia affects my life in a negative way, in the form of altering my sleep cycle. However, I always try to make a positive out of a negative, and I am used to this schedule now. I have actually adapted to my insomnia, and I have found some interesting shows on television, so that staying up is more pleasant lately. Accepting who I am is much more healthy for me than literally forcing myself to remain in bed, while staring at the ceiling. For example, the time is exactly 2:32 am, and I am pleased to be writing to you. I do fall asleep in the form of short cat-naps during the day, and this is all I need to be more refreshed for that specific day.

In conclusion, I wanted to give you, the reader, an up and close personal experience about everything I have been through, from when I was a young girl up through my adult life. I still stumble upon some rough patches, however, I am full of love and joy lately, and I look forward to living each and every day, with the best of intentions. I want to thank God for His love and compassion, which has been the cornerstone of my ability to manage my life so well lately.

Whether it has been encountering: growing up schizophrenic, addicted to a painkiller, rehabilitation, introduction to antipsychotic medication and living through various psychotic events, I have learned that I can get through anything. I revealed myself totally to you, and I was ready to do so from the very first day that I picked up my pen, and started writing this book.

When I was searching for this type of book about fifteen years ago, written not only about schizophrenia but by a schizophrenic person, I could not find anything of this sort. Whether it is being able to feel free on a zip-line, or able to travel without so much psychosis, I realize that the power of my medications are working in my mind beautifully, in order to help me live a more fulfilled life. Also, I cannot reiterate my doctor-patient relationship with Dr. Sloan enough, because he has been my backbone throughout these fifteen years and given me the best advice I could have ever wanted. There are many wonderful books about schizophrenia out on the market, however this one is just a little different. This book was a complete pleasure to write, and I hope to follow this book up with another.

CHAPTER 8
VIGNETTES

This next collection of short stories are thoughtfully written by some of my friends that attend our schizophrenics anonymous meetings. I asked them to share their most intimate thoughts on paper, and they certainly came through. Thanks to each of you, for your efforts in expressing your stories so honestly. I am sure that my readers will connect with many different parts of your stories.

This is "Dora's" story:

Coming from parents who suffer with schizophrenia, alcoholism, and bipolar illness, Dora is plagued with major clinical depression and panic attacks, even as a young girl. She is a very warm and caring individual, who has deep religious beliefs and loves her fellow man. Unfortunately, at three years of age, Dora was molested for the first time, and then molested at least once a year after that, by her uncle.

She is the second child born out of six children, and was very shy and withdrawn as she grew up. All of Dora's nieces and nephews have some sort of a mental illness. As a matter of fact, Dora did not speak for six months, after the shock she endured during the first molestation, when she was just three years of age.

Dora's father used to drink alcohol excessively, and that would use up the money which was intended to pay for the family's necessities for that week. He was a very unstable man, because when he drank, he was mean, hurtful and called Dora dumb and stupid, amongst other adjectives. Although, when he was not drunk, he was basically a nice person. Dora was so shy in school, that she would gladly take an F for any oral assignment given to her, because speaking in front of the class was torture.

Raped at twelve years of age, Dora climbed even more into her shell. However, she was a bit lucky, because she had a best friend and they were inseparable. Both of them would try and protect the other, whenever it was necessary. Dora's parents divorced when she was just fifteen years old. Her mother was a God-fearing woman, who tried to stay married to her husband, but she found out that this was indeed impossible, due to his active alcoholism. Dora's mother had a psychotic breakdown when Dora was fifteen years old.

Her mother was transferred to a psychiatric ward in the local hospital. Dora's mother's mind was not exactly on getting any better in the psychiatric ward, because all of her mind was totally on romancing one of the patients at the hospital. Both Dora's mother and her new beau, thought that the FBI was after them, and they were in a cat and mouse chase together; this seemed exciting to them.

Dora herself met someone romantically, after being shuffled from one foster home to another. Dora, having to change foster homes so frequently, was due to her mother's long stay in the psychiatric ward. Dora was happy at this point in her life, and she decided to get married to the man she loved, and have the baby she was pregnant with.

Unfortunately, she was not pregnant by her husband though. Her pregnancy occurred before she met her husband. When she was at a neighborhood bar one night, someone had slipped a drug into her drink and then raped her. As a result, Dora became pregnant. Her new husband wanted an abortion for her pregnancy immediately, however, Dora said that she wanted to keep the baby. Well, her new husband started beating her in the stomach, while she was pregnant, and he was very verbally and physically abusive towards her. By this time, her father was drinking much more heavily, and her mother, who was back home, was basically staring into space due to all of the medications she was on. In fact, her mother barely recognized Dora. Her father finally died when she was a teenager, and sadness filled her heart.

Dora started having flashbacks in her late teens; it was post-traumatic stress disorder, diagnosed by a physician. Dora, her husband, and the baby boy moved down to Florida because they were very poor, and could not afford housing on their own. Dora's husband found out that there were some good jobs down in Florida, and the rents were cheaper than they were in Connecticut. So, finally after landing in Florida, the three of them were able to live and rent a small room in another person's home, and as a result, they were able to save for an apartment of their own. Dora's husband got much more abusive however, and he ran off romantically with all of her friends, one by one, as she was locked in their apartment all day long.

After eight years of marriage, her husband allowed her to get a waitressing job, and Dora happened to fall in love with the cook at the restaurant; his name was Joe. Joe came to Dora's husband's house one night, and told her husband that he was going to lose something very special, meaning Dora, if he did not get his act together. Dora's husband went to hit her at that moment, and she said that he could not hurt her anymore than he had already done, so she actually gave him permission to hit her again. That day, her husband did not hit her, and that was the turning point of their marriage. Dora felt empowered, and was able to garner a divorce from her husband. Unfortunately, her husband committed suicide after the divorce.

Dora's son was diagnosed with manic depression, and post traumatic stress disorder.

They were so poor in Florida, that they actually made a Christmas tree out of cardboard.

Dora was still falling head over heels in love with the cook at the restaurant she worked at.

She could not sleep at night for a long time, and she could not keep this façade up about loving Joe from afar. One day, she came into the restaurant where she worked, began to cry, and belted out that she was indeed so in love with Joe, that it actually hurt. This is the release that she needed.

Joe reciprocated, and had Dora and her son move in with him, which was in Joe's father's house. As she tells it, Dora and Joe were such good friends by now that, they ended up marrying each other. Still to this day, Dora does not know if this relationship was more of a friendship or a love affair, but they did end up living with Joe's father for the next seven years, however. Joe's alcoholic twin brother also came to live with them for two years, and Dora's father-in-law started to pick on Dora relentlessly, probably due to misplaced anger from his alcoholic son to Dora.

This was very uncomfortable for Dora, so the three of them (Joe, Dora, and her son) moved out and got their own places; Joe in one apartment and Dora and her son in another apartment. Dora went into a deep depression and as a result she could not even drive. Joe never spoke to her about his emotions, and therefore, communication started to break down quickly. Dora and her son ended up moving back to Connecticut for two years, because Joe started an affair with his boss's wife in Florida which crushed Dora. Dora's son was now twenty years old and began experimenting with drugs in 1995, during their time in Connecticut. Dora and Joe talked about wanting to work on their marriage via phone conversations, so Dora and her son moved back down to Florida where Joe was.

Dora's son landed a dream job in North Carolina a couple of months later, but became very depressed during that time, and could not work well, while he was depressed. As a result, Dora's son had to move back to Florida, because he had no steady income, due to his boss firing him. All three of them, at this time, were struggling with their own depressions, and trying their best in order to cope with their illnesses. In addition, Joe was flirting with the mail lady, which actually drove Dora and Joe apart for the last time.

There was lots of anger in their house, and the family literally began to dissolve. Dora, again, was experiencing post-traumatic stress disorder and as a result, Joe and Dora agreed to split up for good. Lately, Dora has been in a depression for over one year, and she has been on medications such as: Valium, Inderal, Librex, Elavil, Paxil, Zoloft, and now she is on, Celexa and Klonopin. This seems to be working for her at the moment, she stated to me.

This is "Steve's" story:

Constantly moving around from place to place as a child, allowed Steve to develop very few friends and a feeling of loneliness. Steve instead worked hard labor for his alcoholic father, when he was only seven years old. He was very uncomfortable and angry when he told me his sad story. Steve's story is one of hard work and abuse. His mother acted very child-like and so Steve lived in a truly patriarch-dominated family, as his father always ran the household. Obliging his father, he drank his first alcoholic beverage at six years old in a bar. Steve made his father very proud of him, just because he drank with the guys. After that incident, Steve drank alcoholic beverages consistently, and was considered an alcoholic by the age of fifteen. He was scared of his father, felt extremely lonely and began experiencing psychoses around this time.

One month later, Steve stated that he no longer suffered with psychoses and he was thrilled with this development. He tried so hard to tell his parents about his journey of psychoses and his head being very foggy, but no one would listen to him. His parents did not want to face what had actually happened to him. Steve thought of himself as an extremely strong individual, due to all of the labor-intensive work he had done as a child and as a teenager. At eighteen years old, his father gave him a tire business of his own.

Steve's schizophrenia started when he was just eighteen years old. His father was a communist and therefore dealt with some shady characters for most of his life. The way Steve tells it, is that he felt dumb from the schizophrenia he had, and so he started dabbling in mind control, getting in touch with his primordial instinct, and lastly, becoming spiritual.

Steve was trying his best to convince me that mind control was a reality, while I was taking his interview down. He swore to me that he could look at his father, and know exactly what was going to happen next.

Trying to forget his anger about his father, who actually ruined his childhood, Steve did some Chi, and other relaxation exercises, otherwise he stated that he could have ripped his father apart and killed him. The young child which remained in him, did not want to harm his father though. Supposedly, with his mind control working, he did not feel the urge to kill his father. Steve told me that he felt as if he were in a hypnotic state many times, due to his schizophrenia.

Becoming more and more numb, due to the feeling of apathy because of his schizophrenia, he applied to work at Electric Boat. This seemed to help him immensely.

Steve believed that a man was measured by how hard he worked. He only worked there for three months, and he seriously thought of giving back the money that he had earned at Electric Boat, because he felt as though he did not work hard enough for his paycheck.

So, Steve went back to work at his tire shop and made some good money, while working hard, which is what he enjoyed.

Having a difficult time remembering who he was and what he stood for, Steve was constantly saying to himself, " If I was myself, I would do and think this way versus that way". He was trying to find his way back into his mind, which is the same kind of feeling that I get when I go out of my body, and I try to get the essence of my soul and mind, back into my body. He was able to think of his father, however, the thoughts were all in a type of flashback mode, because he really did not remember his childhood hardly at all. I do not know if he blocked out his entire childhood, or if this was due to his schizophrenia.

At nineteen years old, Steve decided to go see a psychiatrist, and he told the doctor that there was something wrong with his memory. He stated that he needed some hypnosis to cure him and wanted to be at peace with his father. Steve said that right then and there, he had a spiritual awakening. The psychiatrist diagnosed Steve with severe emotional problems, and schizoaffective disorder. As a result, he had to go into a psychiatric ward in order to deal with these complicated issues. He was placed on Elavil, Trilafon, and later some Prolixin shots. Steve stated to me that he could not sleep for a year straight and this was both terrifying and painful. He had no strength and no energy. Being put on Mellaril in the hospital, and staying away from his parents for approximately six months, made him feel quite a bit better however.

Deciding to go off of the Mellaril, Steve stated that the medication started to hurt him more than help him. The staff at the hospital discharged Steve when the psychiatrist said that he could leave, and his parents let him move into their basement as a temporary shelter.

Now, Steve sees a psychologist at the Christian Counseling Center, he has his own apartment, and he is on his medications daily. Sometimes when he does go off of his medications, he wanders the streets however. He has a good job now, and he is very proud of himself. Currently, Steve is on Geodon, Lexapro, Klonopin, Imipramine, and Risperdal.

All in all, this was a very intense interview; it was raw with emotion and his voice absolutely captured that. Steve has been diagnosed with schizoaffective disorder and major clinical depression.

This is "Linda's" story:

When Linda was a baby, just born, her mother had post-partum depression. When Linda's mother was young herself, she was beat on the head at three years old because Linda's grandmother also suffered from post-partum depression. Linda is the oldest of five children, and no one else has any mental illnesses in her family, except for her and her alcoholic father. She constantly has auditory hallucinations, but does not suffer with visual hallucinations. In first grade, she was sleepwalking and sleep talking. Linda's mother blames Linda's schizophrenia on Linda herself; she has been diagnosed with paranoid schizophrenia. Her mother was very uninvolved with raising her children because she actually treated them just as if they were dolls. Linda's mother had no compassion, especially when Linda was hearing all kinds of voices and sounds. When Linda was young, she had a giant spider hallucination at night, and she would have to face it straight on practically every night. How scary for a young child to deal with this hallucination.

Linda ended up going to the hospital five different times for psychotic episodes. The first time she went, she remained in the psychiatric ward for four months. She was on Prolixin back then. At thirty-three years old, Linda started drinking, and when Linda drank, she was able to speak more freely and more fluently in front of people in general. As a result, she would find herself mostly drinking at family functions and parties.

Hearing voices and questions in her head, Linda started to answer them and then she could not understand what reality was anymore. It was either her own voice, or voices in her head, which confused her immensely. Sometimes, she could understand what reality was and then she would lose the ability to understand what reality is. Is it her imagining the voices, or are they really there?

Linda's parents definitely believe, one hundred percent, that she could get better on her own. She has been seeing the same psychiatrist for twenty years and the last five years, she has been on Haldol, and Zyprexa to control her voices and the negative symptoms that come along with being a paranoid schizophrenic.

I happen to feel closest to Linda's story, because I myself am a paranoid schizophrenic and voices do tend to bother me also. Linda is a very courageous and thoughtful person, and was kind enough to grant me this interview.

This is "Kevin's" story:

Kevin is one of five children, and was born on Long Island in 1952. Even though his father was an active alcoholic, Kevin stated that his life was basically normal until the age of nine. At the age of nine, for example, Kevin's mother would ask him to go to the local package store, in order to stop his father from purchasing more alcohol. Well, Kevin showed up in the store and begged his father not to buy more alcohol. As a result, Kevin was told to go home immediately, and never to bother his father again.

In 1960, Kevin's father's business was doing well, and the family was able to purchase a home in Fairfield, Connecticut. Due to his dyslexia, Kevin had to repeat the fifth grade, and as a result, he was not happy in Connecticut. When he reached the eighth grade, Kevin asked his parents if he could go to a Marine Academy in order to finish his studies. Kevin realized that he needed the discipline that the Academy would provide to him, because he happened to fall in with the so-called undesirable crowd at his public school. The reason for going to the Academy specifically, was that he had earned a suspension from his public school for smoking cigarettes in the lavatory, and all because he wanted to fit in with the cool crowd. In alcoholism, people pleasing is a trait, and Kevin was already showing these signs, as a youngster. Kevin did end up going to the Academy in order to finish his eighth grade studies, however.

When Kevin finished the eighth grade and asked his parents to go away to another military school, his parents said yes. He played soccer, stayed out of trouble for the next four years, and graduated from the military high school there. He got a delayed admission into Manhattenville College, in which the experience of college was uneventful for Kevin.

Studying was always difficult for him, due to his dyslexia, however, he did manage to study philosophy in college. During Kevin's last year in college, he had his first psychotic breakdown. He was suicidal, and remained in the psychiatric ward for two months. He was given so much Thorazine, that the medication made him extremely sleepy. Kevin was eventually diagnosed with manic depression (bipolar illness).

After he was diagnosed with manic depression, he remained in the hospital for an extra nine months. Kevin's father was also a manic depressive. So, after Kevin left the hospital, he and his father were both given a separate recommendation for a specific psychiatrist for each of them, in order to keep both of them in control of their illness.

By this time, Kevin was drinking quite a bit and enjoying himself; he had time to drink because he had not worked for some time.

After graduating from college, he was not able to land a job for about a year and this is the year that he unfortunately drank very heavily. After that year was over, Kevin was able to obtain a job. Kevin had always been interested in how people make paper, and so he became a paper salesman working for a broker. This job lasted for approximately five years; he was so good at his job that the company gave him the best accounts and as a result, he was able to make some adequate income. Kevin's manic depression came back and he became very depressed, and so his psychiatrist placed him on a strong antidepressant and lithium. Kevin still kept getting highs and lows, psychoses, and hypermania. He had grandiose ideas about himself, but nothing he needed to be hospitalized for, just yet.

In 1977, he stopped drinking after a blackout he had experienced. During the blackout, he urinated all over his mother's dresser and mirror during the middle of the night, but when he awoke the following morning, he could not remember anything about the night before. In 1981, the alcoholism started up again; the social drinker suddenly became an alcoholic. Kevin, a manic depressive, had no thoughts of denying his difficult condition. Kevin listened to his psychiatrist and when his doctor stated to him that there should be no more drinking, there was no more drinking. He found it quite easy to quit drinking when he really needed to. His mother and father finally divorced and Kevin stayed sober for five years. Alcoholism and mental illness were two illnesses too tough for Kevin to handle at once, so he started drinking again after about five years of sobriety.

Kevin started going to Alcoholic Anonymous meetings, and they have been helping him stay sober. Kevin found religion in 1980, and that has also helped him to remain sober.

Then, one day Kevin decided to stop taking his antipsychotic medications, and went into full blown psychosis. He had a delusion that the world was going to end, and that Russia was responsible for this. At first, he heard fire trucks, and then he wanted to negotiate peace with Russia, in order to save the world. To do this important mission, Kevin took out a map and saw that Alaska was very close to Russia, and he thought that the Russians would move across the Bering Strait, and start bombing the United States this way. The world was coming to an end, unless Kevin could stop it.

There was a relief organization and he asked to be put through, on the phone, to Israel and then to the Vatican City. He actually asked for the Pope, however, the Pope was sleeping at the time. Kevin's important message was not getting through. By this time, his panic had subsided. Kevin also had another delusion while he remained off of his medications. He thought that it was to late to save anyone else from the destruction that was about to happen due to Russia, so instead, he would just save himself. All of a sudden, he wanted to go to the west coast to find himself. During this manic phase, another place he decided to go to if he could, would be to drive and fly from Hudson Bay to Greenland and Iceland, and thought that he would be safe there. All this was happening on Christmas Eve.

Kevin started driving recklessly and hallucinating when he saw Pegasus coming out of the sky. Kevin thought that he was God's messenger. Kevin chased the hallucination, pulled over in his car, and peeled off all of his clothing. A New York State Trooper stopped him because he had been on the New York City thruway all along. Kevin explained everything to the trooper, which landed Kevin back in the psychiatric hospital for about two weeks. Kevin went back on his psychiatric medications in the hospital and became well again. Kevin has had more episodes like the one I have described, but only when he went off of his medications. The most recent episode has been about God destroying the world.

In 1993, Kevin started working as a rehabilitation counselor. In 1991, he started a schizophrenics anonymous meeting, since he was getting much better by taking his medications and becoming sober. Kevin is now on Depakote and Zyprexa and he feels wonderful. He does not plan to go off of his medications anytime soon.

Family Interviews

These two interviews were written by my husband and mother. I wanted their opinions on how they felt about their relative who lives with a mental illness daily. Thankyou for being heartfelt and straightforward, because I know that this was not an easy task that I asked both of you to complete.

This is my husbands' story:

> I am Nicole's husband, and I could tell that Nicole had an anxiety problem as soon as I met her. However, I had no idea how deeply her mental illness truly went. This is primarily because she was always a good student in school, despite her ferocious migraines, which would often last for days at a time. During her third year of podiatric medical school, I suggested that she take a semester off in order to take care of herself. She always seemed anxious to me, as though she was trying to keep some sort of secret away from everyone. I questioned her, however, the answer was always the same, that she was just working hard and nothing else was bothering her.
>
> I thought that since her headaches made her weak, that she should not try to obtain a surgical residency at the end of her fourth year. Well, she did not listen to me, and went full steam ahead, and obtained that illusive surgical residency for herself. As a result, Nicole had some type of breakdown in her second year surgical residency. Now we know, that it was a psychotic break, but at the time, we were not

sure why she walked off of her job at the hospital. I was just devastated. I wanted her to go back to work the following Monday in the worse way. Nicole had come all of this way, and why would she quit now?

I did not understand and I was so confused.

At this point, I realized that this could be a mentally related illness, maybe brought on by the intense workload at the hospital. The biggest struggle was then to convince her, to seek some professional help from a psychiatrist. I tried many times telling her over and over again that she needed professional help, however, she stated that she was just too embarrassed to tell anyone anything for now. When one day, I was amazed, she just picked up the phone on her own, looked in the yellow pages under psychiatry, and actually called the phone number to a psychiatrist's office. God must have been watching over her. I was not so surprised, when the psychiatrist diagnosed her with paranoid schizophrenia a few months later. After I heard that she had schizophrenia, I spent many nights on the computer trying to understand this complicated illness.

Two years after Nicole saw this psychiatrist, his treatment regimen finally began to work on her. Now, my problem is dealing with the stigma of being married to a mentally ill spouse. Not being able to be honest with my friends, and some family members has been very difficult for me. I had to learn to keep her illness a secret, from basically everyone. I even noticed that Nicole's health care providers treated her differently after they learned of her illness. Nicole, I am always on your side and you are doing great now. I love you so much.

This is my mother's story:

Mental illness is the best-kept secret in our society. No one wants to talk about it or hear of it. If a child or adult is diagnosed with a serious physical illness, that person and family receive sympathy and the benefit of support, but mention your child has a mental illness and the silence is deafening. Most people deal with a mentally ill person by avoiding the subject all together.

When my daughter was first diagnosed with schizophrenia, we were both in complete denial, it had to be a misdiagnosis. We referred to the illness as the S disease, because we could not say the word schizophrenia. It had too many stigmas, and it also hurt too much.

We were devastated. We experienced a severe period of loss, grief, mourning, and anger.

It took me a long time to share this diagnosis with family and just a few friends.

Fortunately, they were very supportive. Once a person declares that he or she has a mental illness, then everything that individual says or does is suspect; this should not be. No one questions how a physically ill person acts, but a person with a mental illness is accountable for all of his or her actions.

In September 2001, I saw a notice in the newspaper about Family to Family classes at N.A.M.I.; it was to last twelve consecutive weeks. I learned so much during my sessions at N.A.M.I.; I cannot praise this organization enough. At first, I blamed myself for not recognizing Nicole's vague symptoms as she was growing up. She was very bright and excelled at everything she did. In my group, were parents, siblings, and consumers.

We soon formed a closely knit family amongst ourselves, along with our two outstanding facilitators. I learned so much from N.A.M.I., I highly recommend this organization.

At N.A.M.I, some of us experienced a test lasting about thirty seconds. This test consisted of what a person with schizophrenia goes through on a daily basis. We were shown a geometric drawing for a few seconds, then asked to repeat that drawing exactly, all the while listening to five different voices whispering in our ears. The whispering was about threats to our lives, the weather, and evil things to horrible to describe, all at the same time. It was an unbelievable experience and impossible to concentrate enough to replicate the geometric drawing exactly. This was an extremely mind boggling experience, which left me numb and near tears.

To the consumers, I would like to say, be as positive as you can, and get help. To the family and friends; encourage your loved one. Receive him or her with open arms. Treat them as you would if they suffered from a medical illness instead of a mental illness.

Above all pray, because God knows that we are all different and have our own mission in this life.

AUTHOR BIOGRAPHY

Nicole Levesque, DPM, was a podiatrist and surgeon from Long Island, New York. She has struggled with schizophrenia all her life but was too scared of being committed to a mental hospital by a psychiatrist. When she was thirty-five, Nicole finally made her first appointment and has since learned to be hopeful about her illness.

Due to a breakdown, Nicole has been unable to work for the past fifteen years, but she enjoys spending time with her loving husband of twenty-four years and writing to help others understand the illness.

Made in the USA
Middletown, DE
05 November 2020